Among Stones

Carol Feller

AMONG STONES

COPYRIGHT © 2013 CAROL FELLER
PHOTOGRAPHY COPYRIGHT © 2013 JOSEPH FELLER
ALL RIGHTS RESERVED.

PUBLISHED BY STOLEN STITCHES
HTTP://WWW.STOLENSTITCHES.COM

ISBN: 978-0-9571212-2-5 (PAPERBACK)

Dacite Page 2

Pyrite Page 6

Liathite Page 10

Liathite Jr Page 16

Tourmalite Page 22

Basanite Page 26

Gabbro Page 32
Techniques 48

Serpentinite Page 40

Dolmite Page 44
Abbreviations 52

Dacite

Dacite

Simple and stylish, this cardigan can be worn open with a draped front or crossed over and buttoned to stay cosy. Knitted from the top down in one piece this cardigan is fast to knit with minimal finishing.

SIZE

To fit actual bust circumference up to:
30 (33, 35, 38, 42, 46, 48, 51)" /
76 (84, 89, 96.5, 106.5, 117, 122, 129.5) cm.
2" / 5 cm of positive ease recommended.

FINISHED MEASUREMENTS

Bust Circumference: 32 (34.75, 37.75, 41.5, 44.25, 48, 50.75, 53.75)" / 81.5 (88.5, 96, 105.5, 112.5, 122, 129, 136.5) cm, with front bands overlapped & buttoned

Length: 21.75 (22.25, 23, 23.25, 23.75, 24.25, 24.75, 25)" / 55 (56.5, 58.5, 59, 60.5, 61.5, 63, 63.5) cm, measured down the back.
Note: This does not include Garter Stitch Collar. Size 37.75" / 96 cm modeled with approx. 3" / 7.5 cm of positive ease.

MATERIALS

Yarn
Studio Donegal 'Soft Donegal' (100% Wool, 190 m / 210 yds per 100g); color: #5202 (Olive Green): 6 (6, 7, 7, 8, 9, 9, 10) skeins.

Needles & Notions
US size 8 / 5mm circular needle, 40"/ 100cm long (*or longer for bigger sizes*)
1 set US size 8 / 5mm double-point needles (*if magic loop is not used for sleeves*)

Always use a needle size that gives you the gauge listed, as every knitter's gauge is unique.

Stitch markers; waste yarn; tapestry needle; 2 buttons approx 1"/ 2.5 cm diameter.

GAUGE

17 sts / 24 rows = 4" / 10 cm in st st
17 sts / 32 rows = 4" / 10 cm in garter st

PATTERN NOTES

See techniques section on page 48: Garter Stitch in Rows, Garter Stitch in Rnds, Single Row Buttonhole, Backwards Loop Cast On, Cable Cast On, Provisional Cast On, I-cord Bind Off, Grafting & Short Rows.

PATTERN

This cardigan is worked from the top down, starting with the collar. Raglan shoulder shaping is worked in one piece.

COLLAR
With circ needle using Provisional Cast On & waste yarn, CO 96 (98, 100, 106, 112, 118, 124, 130) sts.
Do not join.
With working yarn, knit one row.
Next Row: Knit to last 3 sts, sl 3 wyif.
Rep this row until work meas approx 5 (5, 5.5, 5.5, 6, 6, 6.5, 6.5)" / 12.5 (12.5, 14, 14, 15, 15, 16.5, 16.5) cm.
Next Row (RS): K61 (63, 65, 69, 73, 77, 81, 85) sts, w&t.
Next Row (WS): K26 (28, 30, 32, 34, 36, 38, 40) sts, w&t.
Next Row: Knit to previous wrapped st, knit wrap with stitch, k1, w&t.
Rep this row 5 more times.
Work RS row to end of row, knitting wrapped st tog with wrap.

Next Row (WS): Knit to last 3 sts, knitting wrapped st tog with wrap, sl 3 wyif.

YOKE
Set-up Row (RS): K28 (28, 30, 32, 34, 36, 38, 40), kfb, pm, kfb, k4 (4, 2, 2, 2, 2, 2, 2), kfb, pm, kfb, k24 (26, 28, 30, 32, 34, 36, 38), kfb, pm, kfb, k4 (4, 2, 2, 2, 2, 2, 2), kfb, pm, kfb, knit to last 3 sts, sl 3 wyif.
104 (106 108, 114, 120, 126, 132, 138) sts – *8 sts inc'd.*
Next Row (WS & all WS): Knit to one st before first m, purl to last m, sl m, p1, knit to last 3 sts, sl 3 wyif.
Buttonhole Row (RS): [Knit to one st before m, kfb, sl m, kfb] four times, k6, work Single Row Buttonhole, knit to last 10 sts, work Single Row Buttonhole, knit to last 3 sts, sl 3 wyif. - *8 sts inc'd.*
Work one WS row.
Raglan Increase Row (RS): [Knit to one st before m, kfb, sl m, kfb] four times, knit to last 3 sts, sl 3 wyif. - *8 sts inc'd.*
Work one WS row.
Rep last two rows 17 (19, 21, 22, 23, 25, 26, 27) more times. 256 (274, 292, 306, 320, 342, 356, 370) total sts; 49 (51, 55, 58, 61, 65, 68, 71) sts for each front, 46 (50, 52, 54, 56, 60, 62, 64) sts for each sleeve, 66 (72, 78, 82, 86, 92, 96, 100) sts for back.

Sleeve Dividing Row (RS): *Knit to m, remove m, sl next 46 (50, 52, 54, 56, 60, 62, 64) sts (all sts to next m) to waste yarn, remove m, using backward loop method, CO 2 (2, 2, 6, 8, 10, 12, 14) sts, place m at center of cast-on sts; rep from * once more, knit to last 3 sts, sl 3 wyif. 168 (178, 192, 210, 224, 242, 256, 270) sts.

BODY
Next Row (WS): Knit to last st before m, p1, sl m, purl to m, sl m, p1, knit to last 3 sts, sl 3 wyif.
Next Row (RS): Knit to last st before m, sl 1 p-wise wyib, sl m, knit to last m, sl m, sl 1 p-wise wyib, knit to last 3 sts, sl 3 wyif.
Work in patt est'd until work measures approx 2" / 5 cm (meas at back) from underarm, ending with a RS row.
Next Row (WS): Knit to last st before m, p1, sl m, p22 (24, 26, 29, 31, 34, 36, 38), place dart m (dm), p24 (26, 28, 30, 32, 34, 36, 38), place dart m, purl to m, sl m, p1, knit to last 3 sts, sl 3 wyif.
Waist Dec Row (RS): Knit to last st before m, sl 1 p-wise wyib, sl m, *knit to 2 sts before dm, k2tog, sl m, ssk; rep from * once more, knit to last m, sl m, sl 1 p-wise wyib, knit to last 3 sts, sl 3 wyif. *4 sts dec'd.*
Work Waist Dec Row every 8th row four more times. 148 (158, 172, 190, 204, 222, 236, 250) sts.
Work even in patt for 9 rows ending with a WS row.
Hip Inc Row (RS): Knit to last st before m, sl 1 p-wise wyib, sl m, *knit to 1 st before dm, M1R, k1, sl m, k1, M1L; rep from * once, knit to last m, sl m, sl 1 p-wise wyib, knit to last 3 sts, sl 3 wyif. - *4 sts inc'd.*
Work Hip Inc Row every 4th row four more times. 168 (178, 192, 210, 224, 242, 256, 270) sts.
Work even in patt until body meas approx 13" / 33 cm (meas at back) from underarm ending with a WS row.

Hem
Next Row: Knit to last 3 sts, sl 3 wyif.
Rep this row until hem measures approx 2" / 5 cm, ending with a WS row.
BO to last 3 sts using I-cord bind off, note that first 3 sts (I-cord) are used to begin BO. When 3 sts remain on each needle graft start and end of I-cord tog.

SLEEVES
Using dpns or long circ with magic loop, starting at center of underarm, pick up and knit 1 (1, 1, 3, 4, 5, 6, 7) sts along CO underarm edge, k46 (50, 52, 54, 56, 60, 62, 64) held sleeve sts, pick up and knit 1 (1, 1, 3, 4, 5, 6, 7) sts along remaining half of CO underarm edge. Join to work in the rnd. 48 (52, 54, 60, 64, 70, 74, 78) sts.
Knit 18 (12, 12, 8, 8, 6, 5, 5) rnds.
Sleeve Dec Rnd: K2tog, knit to last 2 sts, ssk.
2 sts dec'd.
Rep these 19 (13, 13, 9, 9, 7, 6, 6) rnds 3 (5, 5, 8, 8, 11, 12, 14) more times. 40 (40, 42, 42, 46, 46, 48, 48) sts.
Cont in st st until sleeve measures 16 (16, 16.5, 16.5, 17, 17, 17, 17.5)" / 40.5 (40.5, 42, 42, 43, 43, 43, 44.5) cm from underarm or desired length to beginning of garter cuff.

6.75 (7.25, 8, 8.25, 8.75, 9.25, 9.75, 10)" / 17 (18.5, 20.5, 21, 22, 23.5, 25, 25.5) cm

5 (5, 5.5, 5.5, 6, 6, 6.5, 6.5)" / 12.5 (12.5, 14, 14, 15, 15, 16.5, 16.5) cm

6 (6.5, 7, 7.5, 8, 8.5, 9, 9.5)" / 15 (16.5, 18, 19, 20.5, 21.5, 23, 24) cm

11.25 (12.25, 12.75, 14, 15, 16.5, 17.5, 18.25)" / 28.5 (31, 32.5, 35.5, 38, 42, 44.5, 46.5) cm

Back

Waist

Front

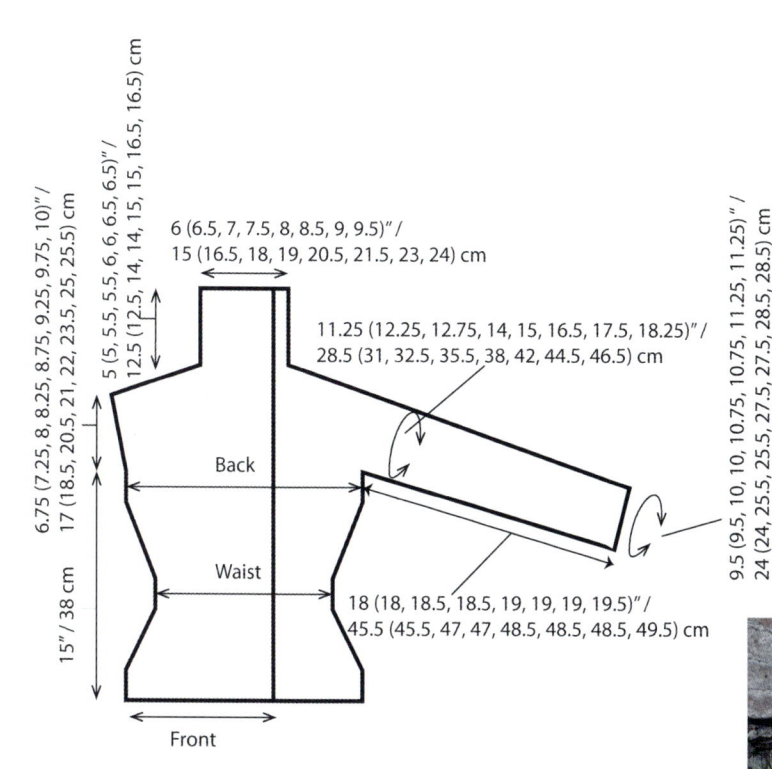

18 (18, 18.5, 18.5, 19, 19, 19, 19.5)" / 45.5 (45.5, 47, 47, 48.5, 48.5, 48.5, 49.5) cm

9.5 (9.5, 10, 10, 10.75, 10.75, 11.25, 11.25)" / 24 (24, 25.5, 25.5, 27.5, 27.5, 28.5, 28.5) cm

15" / 38 cm

Back: 16 (17.5, 18.75, 20.75, 22, 24, 25.5, 26.75)" / 40.5 (44.5, 47.5, 52.5, 56, 61, 65, 68) cm

Waist: 11.25 (12.75, 14, 16, 17.5, 19.25, 20.75, 22)" / 28.5 (32.5, 35.5, 40.5, 44.5, 49, 52.5, 56) cm

Front: 11.75 (12.25, 13.25, 14.25, 15.25, 16.5, 17.5, 18.25)" / 30 (31, 33.5, 36, 38.5, 42, 44.5, 46.5) cm

Work in garter st for 2" / 5 cm.
BO all sts using I-cord bind off.
Work second sleeve in the same way.

FINISHING

Undo Provisional Cast On at collar, placing all sts on circ needle. Work I-cord bind off to last 3 sts, using first 3 sts for I-cord. When 3 sts remain on each needle graft start and end of I-cord together.
Weave in ends.
Sew buttons in position, opposite buttonholes.
Block to dimensions given on schematic.

PYRITE

Pyrite

Worked from the top down, this subtle slip stitch pattern is an ideal way to smoothly blend a variegated yarn or just add a little textural interest to your sock. The texture pattern is subtle enough to make this a great sock pattern for anyone.

Size

Child (Woman's medium, Men's medium)

Finished Measurements

Foot Circumference: 7.25 (8.25, 9.25)" / 18.5 (21, 23.5) cm

Materials

Yarn
Approx Yardage: 250 (360, 420) m / 275 (394, 460) yds
Men's Version: Miss Babs 'Yummy Superwash Sock & Baby Yarn - 2 ply' (100% Merino Wool, 366 m / 400 yds per 113g); color: Prince; 1 (1, 2) skein(s)
Woman's Version: Easy Knits 'Deeply Wicked' (100% Merino Wool, 400 m / 437 yds per 100g); color: Rusting Reef; 1 (1, 2) skein
Child's Version: Alisha Goes Around 'Richness (of Martens) Fingering' (75% Superwash Merino, 15% Cashmere, 10% Silk, 366 m / 400 yds per 115g); color: Naval Campaign; 1 (1, 2) skein(s)

Needles & Notions
US size 1.5 / 2.5mm circular needle 32" / 80 cm long
Markers, tapestry needle.

Gauge

30 sts / 44 rows = 4" / 10 cm in st st
36 sts / 44 rows = 4" / 10 cm in slip stitch patt

Pattern Notes

See techniques section on page 48: Long Tail Cast On & Grafting.

1x1 Ribbing
Rnd 1: *K1, p1; rep from * to end of rnd.
Rep Rnd 1 for patt.

Instep Slip St Pattern
All sts are slipped p-wise wyib.

Child and Men's Size:
Rnd 1: Sl 1, *k3, sl 1; rep from * to last st, k1.
Rnd 2: Sl 1, *p3, sl 1; rep from * to last st, p1.
Rnd 3: K1, *k1, sl 1, k2; rep from * to last st, k1.
Rnd 4: P1, *p1, sl 1, p2; rep from * to last st, p1.
Rep these 4 rnds for patt.

Woman's Size:
Rnd 1: K2, sl 1, *k3, sl 1; rep from * to last 3 sts, k3.
Rnd 2: P2, sl 1, *p3, sl 1; rep from * to last 3 sts, p3.
Rnd 3: Sl1, k2, *k1, sl 1, k2; rep from * to last 3 sts, k1, sl 1, k1.
Rnd 4: Sl1, p2, *p1, sl 1, p2; rep from * to last 3 sts, p1, sl 1, p1.
Rep these 4 rnds for patt.

Pattern

These socks were worked using magic loop technique. If you would rather use dpns or two circ needles, just substitute.

Cuff

CO 60 (68, 76) sts. Ensure you cast on loosely so that the cuff can stretch. It may be necessary to cast on over 2 needles held together in order for it to be loose enough. Long tail cast on works well.
Using magic loop technique, work in 1x1 ribbing until cuff measures approx 1.75" / 4.5 cm.

Leg

Slip St Pattern (multiple of 4 sts)
All sts are slipped p-wise wyib.
Rnd 1: *K3, sl 1; rep from * to end of rnd.
Rnd 2: *P3, sl 1; rep from * to end of rnd.
Rnd 3: *K1, sl 1, k2; rep from * to end of rnd.
Rnd 4: *P1, sl 1, p2; rep from * to end of rnd.
Rep Rnds 1-4 until sock meas approx 5 (5.5, 6)" / 12.5 (14, 15) cm from top of cuff, ending with Rnd 4 of Slip St Patt.

Heel Flap

Heel stitches will be worked flat using the circ needle. Instep stitches will remain at the back on the cable of the circ needle. If you rather, they could be transferred to a holder.
Set-Up Row 1 (RS): K15 (17, 19), turn.
Set-Up Row 2 (WS): Sl 1 p-wise wyif, p29 (33, 37), turn. Sl all other 30 (34, 38) sts to cable of circ needle to be held.
Row 1 (RS): Sl 1 k-wise, *k1, sl 1 p-wise wyib; rep from * to last st, k1, turn.
Row 2 (WS): Sl 1 p-wise wyif, p29 (33, 37), turn.
Rep these two rows 13 (15, 17) more times. You will have 14 (16, 18) edge sl sts.

Turn Heel

Next Row (RS): Sl 1 k-wise, k16 (18, 20), ssk, k1, turn work. 29 (33, 37) total sts rem for heel. 10 (12, 14) sts rem unworked.
Next Row (WS): Sl 1 p-wise, p5, p2tog, p1, turn work. 28 (32, 36) sts.
Next Row (RS): Sl 1 k-wise, k6, ssk, k1, turn. 27 (31, 35) sts.
Next Row (WS): Sl1 p-wise, p7, p2tog, p1, turn. 26 (30, 34) sts.
Next Row (RS): Sl 1 k-wise, k8, ssk, k1, turn. 25 (29, 33) sts.
Next Row (WS): Sl1 p-wise, p9, p2tog, p1, turn. 24 (28, 32) sts.
Next Row (RS): Sl 1 k-wise, k10, ssk, k1, turn. 23 (27, 31) sts.
Next Row (WS): Sl1 p-wise, p11, p2tog, p1, turn. 22 (26, 30) sts.
Next Row (RS): Sl 1 k-wise, k12, ssk, k1, turn. 21 (25, 29) sts.
Next Row (WS): Sl1 p-wise, p13, p2tog, p1, turn. 20 (24, 28) sts.
Next Row (RS): Sl 1 k-wise, k14, ssk, k1, turn. 19 (23, 27) sts.
Next Row (WS): Sl1 p-wise, p15, p2tog, p1, turn. 18 (22, 26) sts.

Woman's & Men's size only:
Next Row (RS): Sl 1 k-wise, k16, ssk, k1, turn. - (21, 25) sts.
Next Row (WS): Sl1 p-wise, p17, p2tog, p1, turn. - (20, 24) sts.

Men's size only:
Next Row (RS): Sl 1 k-wise, k18, ssk, k1, turn. - (-, 23) sts.
Next Row (WS): Sl1 p-wise, p19, p2tog, p1, turn. - (-, 22) sts.

Heel Gusset

Sl 1 k-wise, k17 (19, 21), pick up and knit 15 (17, 19) sts down side of heel flap, turn to work on second side of magic loop, pm, work 30 (34, 38) sts in Instep Slip St Patt (*see pattern notes*), pm, pick up and knit 15 (17, 19) sts down side of heel flap. 78 (88, 98) sts.

Rnd 1: Knit to 3 sts before m, k2tog, k1, sl m, work Instep Slip St Patt to m, sl m, k1, ssk, knit to end. 76 (86, 96) sts.
Rnd 2: Knit to m, sl m, work Instep Slip St Patt to m, sl m, knit to end of rnd.

Rep these two rnds 8 (9, 10) more times. 60 (68, 76) sts.
Reorganise your sts so that 1st side of needle has just 30 (34, 38) sts for sole and 2nd side has 30 (34, 38) sts for instep. Remove markers. Arrange beg of rnd to start of sole sts.
Next Rnd: Knit 1st side, work Instep Slip St patt to end of rnd.
Cont to work this rnd until foot meas approx 6 (7.5, 8)" / 15 (19, 20.5) cm from back of heel.
If you want to adjust foot length work to desired length less 2 (2, 2.25)" / 5 (5, 5.5) cm for toe decreases.

TOE
The toe will be worked in st st.
Rnd 1: K1, ssk, knit to 3 sts before end of 1st side, k2tog, k1; k1, ssk, knit to 3 sts before end of rnd, k2tog, k1. 56 (64, 72) sts.
Rnd 2: Knit.
Rep these two rnds 7 (7, 8) more times. 28 (36, 40) sts.
Rep Rnd 1 only 5 (6, 7) times. 8 (12, 12) sts.
Cut yarn with a long tail, 4 (6, 6) sts will be on needle at each side. Graft stitches together.

FINISHING

Weave in all yarn ends with tapestry needle. Block socks to correct dimensions.

Liathite

Liathite

Keep yourself warm this winter with this fast to knit, flattering hoodie. Casual enough to wear every day, this will be the first garment you'll grab when you leave the house! Knit from the top down in one piece with raglan shoulder shaping.

Sizes

To fit actual bust circumference up to:
31 (35, 37, 41, 44, 47, 50, 53)" /
78.5 (89, 94, 104, 112, 119.5, 127, 134.5) cm
0-2" / 0-5 cm of positive ease recommended.

Finished Measurements

Bust Circumference: 30.5 (34, 36.25, 39.75, 43.25, 45.5, 48.75, 52.25)" / 77.5 (86.5, 92, 101, 110, 115.5, 124, 132.5) cm
Size 34.25" / 87 cm modeled with .5" / 1.5 cm of negative ease.

Length: 22 (22.5, 23.25, 23.5, 24, 24.5, 24.75, 25.5)" / 56 (57, 59, 59.5, 61, 62, 63, 65) cm not including hood

Materials

Yarn

Berroco 'Vintage Chunky' (50% Acrylic, 40% Wool, 10% Nylon; 130 yds / 120 m per 3.5 oz / 100g skein); Color: Smoke (6106); 7 (7, 8, 8, 9, 10, 10, 11) skeins.

Needles & Notions

Size 10 US / 6 mm circular needle, 40" / 100 cm length (or longer, to suit size made)
Size 9 US / 5.5 mm circular needle, 40" / 100 cm length (or longer, to suit size made) for ribbing
1 Size 10 US / 6 mm & 9 US / 5.5 mm dpns (*if magic loop method is not used for sleeves*)

Stitch markers (including 4 split ring), cable needle, waste yarn, tapestry needle, open zip approx. 20 (20, 20, 20.5, 20.5, 21, 21, 22)" / 51 (51, 51, 52, 52, 53.5, 53.5, 56) cm long (or longer, can be cut to length).

Gauge

14 sts / 20 rows = 4" / 10 cm in st st with larger needle
Four Rib Braid chart meas 3" / 7.5cm across with larger needle
18 sts / 22 rows = 4" / 10 cm 2x2 Ribbing (*relaxed*) with smaller needle
Adjust needle size if necessary to obtain correct gauge.

Pattern Notes

See techniques section on page 48: Short Rows, Cable Cast On, Backward Loop Cast On & 3-Needle Bind Off.

Cable Chart & Instructions

2/1/2 RC Sl 3 sts on cn & hold at back of work, k2, sl final p st from cn to LH needle & p, k2 from cn.
2/1 RPC Sl 1 st on cn & hold at back of work, k2, p1 from cn.
2/1 LPC Sl 2 sts on cn & hold at front of work, p1, k2 from cn.
2/2 RC Sl 2 sts on cn & hold at back of work, k2, k2 from cn.
2/2 LC Sl 2 sts on cn & hold at front of work, k2, k2 from cn.
2/1/2 LC Sl 3 sts on cn & hold at front of work, k2, sl final p st from cn to LH needle & p, k2 from cn.

Four Rib Braid
Row 1 (WS): [K2, p2] twice, k1, [p2, k2] twice.
Row 2 (RS): P2, k2, p2, 2/1/2 RC, p2, k2, p2.
Row 3 (WS): [K2, p2] twice, k1, [p2, k2] twice.
Row 4 (RS): P2, 2/1 LPC, 2/1 RPC, p1, 2/1 LPC, 2/1 RPC, p2.
Row 5 (WS): [K3, p4] twice, k3.
Row 6 (RS): P3, 2/2 RC, p3, 2/2 LC, p3.
Row 7 (WS): [K3, p4] twice, k3.
Row 8 (RS): P2, 2/1 RPC, 2/1 LPC, p1, 2/1 RPC, 2/1 LPC, p2.
Row 9 (WS): [K2, p2] twice, k1, [p2, k2] twice.
Row 10 (RS): P2, k2, p2, 2/1/2 LC, p2, k2, p2.
Row 11 (WS): [K2, p2] twice, k1, [p2, k2] twice.
Row 12 (RS): P2, 2/1 LPC, 2/1 RPC, p1, 2/1 LPC, 2/1 RPC, p2.
Row 13 (WS): [K3, p4] twice, k3.
Row 14 (RS): P3, 2/2 RC, p3, 2/2 LC, p3.
Row 15 (WS): [K3, p4] twice, k3.
Row 16 (RS): P2, 2/1 RPC, 2/1 LPC, p1, 2/1 RPC, 2/1 LPC, p2.

PATTERN

Yoke
With larger circ needle, CO 32 (36, 36, 38, 44, 44, 50, 50) sts.
Set-Up Row (WS): P2, pm, p4 (4, 4, 4, 6, 6, 8, 8), pm, p20 (24, 24, 26, 28, 28, 30, 30), pm, p4 (4, 4, 4, 6, 6, 8, 8), pm, p2.
Raglan Inc Row (RS): *Knit to last st before m, M1R, k1, sl m, k1, M1L; rep from * 3 more times, knit to end of row. 40 (44, 44, 46, 52, 52, 58, 58) sts - *8 sts inc'd.*
Next Row (WS & all WS rows): Purl.
Rep these two rows once more. 48 (52, 52, 54, 60, 60, 66, 66) sts.
Neck Inc Row (RS): K1, M1R, *knit to last st before m, M1R, k1, sl m, k1, M1L; rep from * 3 more times, knit to last st, M1L, k1. 58 (62, 62, 64, 70, 70, 76, 76) sts - *10 sts inc'd.*
Work 1 WS row.
Rep these two rows 2 (2, 3, 3, 4, 4, 5, 5) more times. 78 (82, 92, 94, 110, 110, 126, 126) sts.

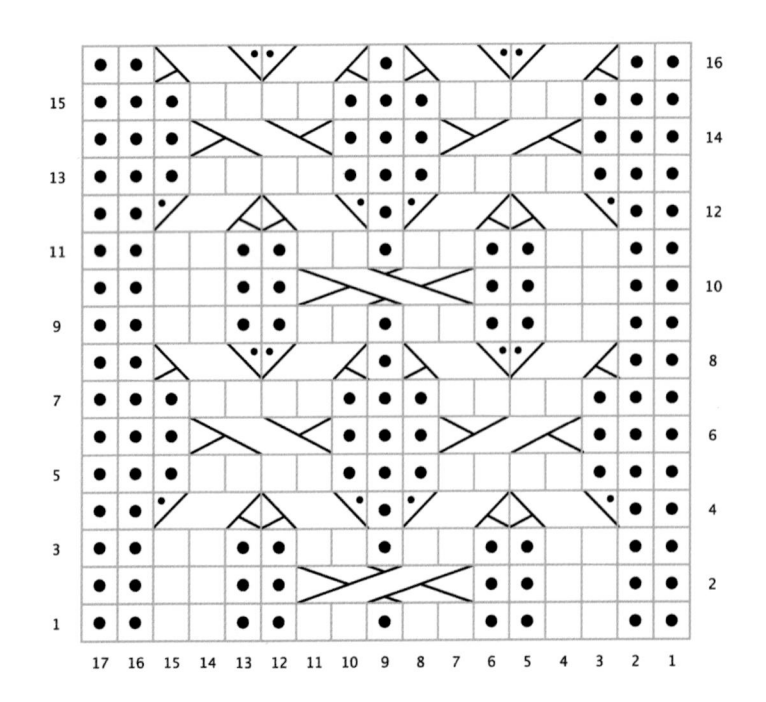

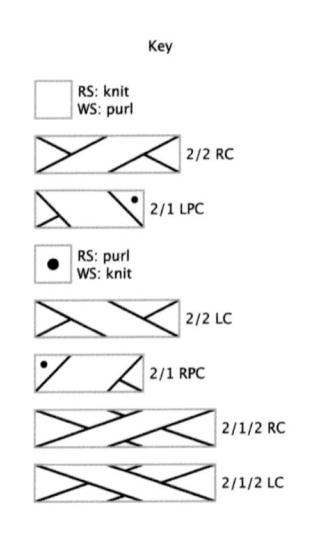

Work RS Neck Inc Row. – 10 sts inc'd.
Neck Inc Row (WS): P1, M1p, purl to last st, M1p, p1.
– 2 sts inc'd.
Rep these two rows once. 102 (106, 116, 118, 134, 134, 150, 150) sts.
Neck Cast On Row (RS): Using Cable Cast On, CO 10 (12, 11, 12, 12, 12, 12, 12) sts, k2, sl 1 p-wise, (p2, k2) twice, p1, (k2, p2) twice, *knit to last st before m, M1R, k1, sl m, k1, M1L; rep from * 3 more times, knit to end of row. 120 (126, 135, 138, 154, 154, 170, 170) sts.
Neck Cast On Row (WS): Using Cable Cast On, CO 10 (12, 11, 12, 12, 12, 12, 12) sts, p3, work Four Rib Braid, purl to last 20 sts, work Four Rib Braid, p3. 130 (138, 146, 150, 166, 166, 182, 182) sts.
Raglan Inc Row (RS): K2, sl 1 p-wise, work Four Rib Braid over next 17 sts, *knit to last st before m, M1R, k1, sl m, k1, M1L; rep from * 3 more times, knit to last 20 sts, work Four Rib Cable, sl 1 p-wise, k2.
Next Row (WS): P3, work Four Rib Braid, purl to last 20 sts, work Four Rib Braid, p3.
Rep these two rows 8 (9, 10, 10, 9, 9, 8, 9) more times. 202 (218, 234, 238, 246, 246, 254, 262) sts.

Yoke for sizes 30.5 (34, 36.25)" / 77.5 (86.5, 92) cm are now complete; proceed to Sleeve Divide Row.

**Sizes - (-, -, 39.75, 43.25, 45.5, 48.75, 52.25)" /
- (-, -, 101, 110, 115.5, 124, 132.5) cm only**
Body Inc Row (RS): *Work in patt to last st before m, M1R, k1, sl m, knit to m, sl m, k1, M1L; rep from * once more, work in patt to end of row. – 4 sts inc'd.
Next Row (WS): Work all sts in patt est'd.
Rep these two rows - (-, -, 0, 1, 2, 3, 4) more times.
- (-, -, 242, 254, 258, 270, 282) sts.

All Sizes
Sleeve Divide Row (RS): *Work in patt to m, remove m, sl 38 (40, 44, 44, 46, 46, 48, 50) sleeve sts to waste yarn, remove m, using Backwards Loop Cast On, CO 0 (0, 0, 1, 2, 3, 4, 5) sts, pm for side seam, CO 0 (0, 0, 1, 2, 3, 4, 5) sts; rep from * once, work in patt to end of row.
126 (138, 146, 158, 170, 178, 190, 202) sts.

BODY
Work even in patt until work measures approx 2" / 5cm from underarm ending with a WS row.
Note: try work on at this point to verify that it reaches approx fullest bust point.

Waist Shaping
Waist Dec Row (RS): *Work in patt to 4 sts before side m, ssk, k2, sl m, k2, k2tog; rep from * once, work in patt to end of row.
122 (134, 142, 154, 166, 174, 186, 198) sts.
Work even in patt until work meas approx 7.5 (7.25, 7, 7, 7, 6.75, 6.25, 6)" / 19 (18.5, 18, 18, 18, 17, 16, 15) cm from underarm ending with a WS row.
Work Waist Dec Row once.
118 (130, 138, 150, 162, 170, 182, 194) sts.
Work 7 rows even in patt.

Hip Shaping
Hip Inc Row (RS): *Work in patt to 2 sts before side m, M1R, k2, sl m, k2, M1L; rep from * once, work in patt to end of row. 122 (134, 142, 154, 166, 174, 186, 198) sts.
Work 5 (5, 7, 7, 7, 7, 9, 9) rows even in patt.
Work Hip Inc Row once more. 126 (138, 146, 158, 170, 178, 190, 202) sts.
Work even in patt until body meas approx 10.5" / 26.5 cm from underarm ending with row 2, 8, 10 or 16 of Four Rib Braid Chart.

Waistband
Set-up Row (WS): With smaller circ needle, p3, [k2, p2] twice, k1, M1, *p2, k2; rep from * to last 12 sts, M1, k1, [p2, k2] twice, p3. 128 (140, 148, 160, 172, 180, 192, 204) sts.
Next Row (RS): K2, sl 1 p-wise, *p2, k2; rep from * to last 5 sts, p2, sl 1, k2.
Next Row (WS): P3, *k2, p2; rep from * to last st, p1.
Work even in patt est'd until body meas approx 15" / 38 cm from underarm.
BO all sts loosely in patt.

SLEEVES

Sleeves will be knit in the round using magic loop or dpns.

With larger circ needle (or dpns), starting at center of underarm, pick up and knit 0 (0, 0, 1, 2, 3, 4, 5) sts, k38 (40, 44, 44, 46, 46, 48, 50) held sleeve sts, pick up and knit 0 (0, 0, 1, 2, 3, 4, 5) sts from underarm, pm for start of rnd, join to work in the rnd. 38 (40, 44, 46, 50, 52, 56, 60) sts.

Knit approx. 6" / 15 cm even from underarm.

Sleeve Dec Rnd: K2tog, knit to last 2 sts, ssk. 36 (38, 42, 44, 48, 50, 54, 58) sts – *2 sts dec'd.*

Rep Sleeve Dec Rnd every 13th (10th, 6th, 8th, 5th, 5th, 5th, 4th) rnd 2 (3, 5, 4, 6, 7, 7, 9) more times. 32 (32, 32, 36, 36, 36, 40, 40) sts.

Knit every rnd until sleeve meas approx. 12.5 (13, 13.25, 13.5, 13.75, 14, 14, 14.5)" / 32 (33, 33.5, 34.5, 35, 35.5, 35.5, 37) cm.

Cuff

With smaller circ needle, *K2, p2; rep from * to end of rnd.

Rep this rnd until Cuff meas approx. 5.5" / 14 cm.

BO all sts in patt loosely.

FINISHING

Hood

Fold front edging along slip st and pin in place to the inside of the work. Note that when picking up sts for hood you will pick up 'double' sts at each edge where sts are folded down.

With RS facing and using smaller circ needle, starting at right side of cast-on neck sts, pick up and knit 7 (9, 8, 9, 9, 9, 9) sts to end of front neck cast on, pick up and knit 12 (12, 15, 15, 16, 16, 17, 19) sts to first cast on edge, pick up and knit 32 (36, 36, 38, 44, 44, 50, 50) sts from cast-on, pick up and knit 12 (12, 15, 15, 16, 16, 17, 19) sts to left front cast-on sts, pick up and knit final 7 (9, 8, 9, 9, 9, 9) sts.
70 (78, 82, 86, 94, 94, 102, 106) sts.

Next Row (WS): *P2, k2; rep from * to last 2 sts, p2.
Next Row (RS): *K2, p2; rep from * to last 2 sts, k2.

For Sizes 30.5 (34, 36.25, 39.75, 43.25, 45.5, -, -)" / 77.5 (86, 92, 101, 110, 115.5, -, -) cm Only

Pm 24 (28, 28, 30, 34, 34, -, -) sts from each end.
Work even in patt for 5 (5, 7, 11, 11, 11, -, -) rows.
Hood Inc Row (RS): Work to m, M1, sl m, work to 2nd m, sl m, M1, work to end of row. – *2 sts inc'd.*
Note: Work M1 as knit or purl as necessary to match pattern.
Rep these 6 (6, 8, 12, 12, 12, -, -) rows 7 (7, 5, 3, 3, 3, -, -) more times. Remove both markers. 86 (94, 94, 94, 102, 102, -, -) sts.

For All Sizes
Work even in patt until hood meas approx. 11" / 28 cm (or desired length) ending with a WS row.
Place marker at center of sts.

Short Row Shaping
Short Row (RS): Work in patt to 4 sts before m, w&t.
Next Row (WS): Work in patt to end of row.
Short Row (RS): Work in patt to 4 sts before previous wrapped st, w&t.
Next Row (WS): Work in patt to end of row.
Rep last two rows 6 (7, 7, 7, 8, 8, 9, 9) more times.
Work to 1 st before m, picking up and working all wraps with st they wrap as you pass them, BO 2 sts (removing center m), work in patt to end of row.
Short Row (WS): Work in patt to 3 sts before BO sts, w&t.
Next Row (RS): Work in patt to end of row.
Short Row (WS): Work in patt to 4 sts before previous wrapped st, w&t.
Next Row (RS): Work in patt to end of row.
Rep last two rows 6 (7, 7, 7, 8, 8, 9, 9) more times.
Turn hood inside out and bind off all sts using 3-needle bind off, taking care to pick up wraps as you pass them.

Sewing Zip in Position

With zip closed, pin each front edge to zip, bringing edges close to teeth without covering. Take care not to

15

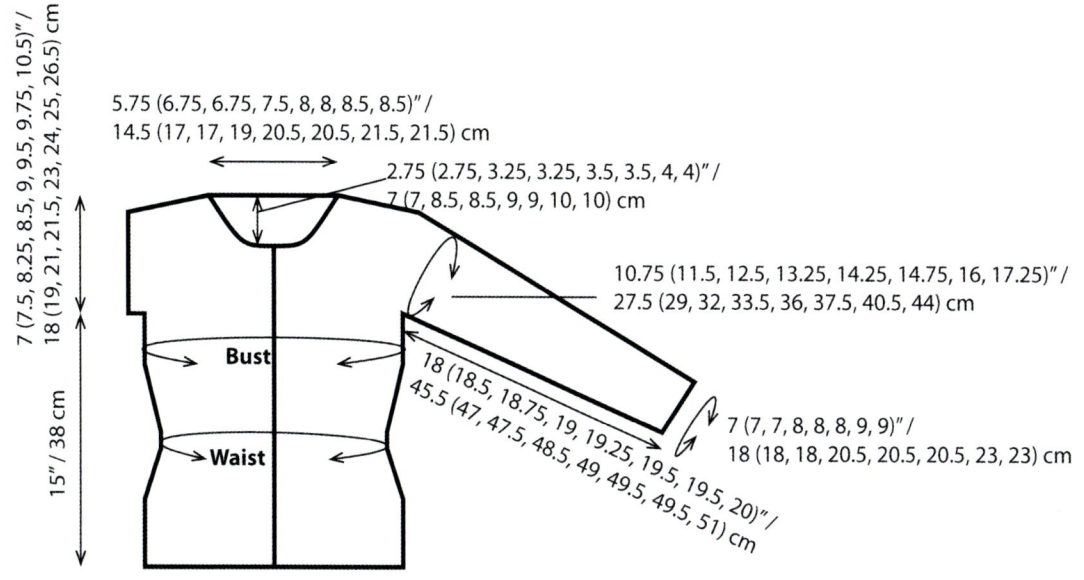

7 (7.5, 8.25, 8.5, 9, 9.5, 9.75, 10.5)" / 18 (19, 21, 21.5, 23, 24, 25, 26.5) cm

5.75 (6.75, 6.75, 7.5, 8, 8, 8.5, 8.5)" / 14.5 (17, 17, 19, 20.5, 20.5, 21.5, 21.5) cm

2.75 (2.75, 3.25, 3.25, 3.5, 3.5, 4, 4)" / 7 (7, 8.5, 8.5, 9, 9, 10, 10) cm

10.75 (11.5, 12.5, 13.25, 14.25, 14.75, 16, 17.25)" / 27.5 (29, 32, 33.5, 36, 37.5, 40.5, 44) cm

18 (18.5, 18.75, 19, 19.25, 19.5, 19.5, 20)" / 45.5 (47, 47.5, 48.5, 49, 49.5, 49.5, 51) cm

7 (7, 7, 8, 8, 8, 9, 9)" / 18 (18, 18, 20.5, 20.5, 20.5, 23, 23) cm

15" / 38 cm

Bust: 30.5 (34, 36.25, 39.75, 43.25, 45.5, 48.75, 52.25)" / 77.5 (86.5, 92, 101, 110, 115.5, 124, 132.5) cm
Waist: 28.25 (31.75, 34, 37.5, 40.75, 43.25, 46.5, 50)" / 72 (80.5, 86.5, 95.5, 103.5, 110, 118, 127) cm

stretch knitting. Note that the front edges are folded under at the sl st row. If zip is longer than opening, cut at top to length and fold edge down. Open zip and sew front edges of cardigan in place as close to teeth as possible.

Now working from inside, sew other edge of the zip in position. Ensure that stitches can't be seen from front of work.

Weave in loose ends using tapestry needle. Sew underarm seams if necessary. Block to dimensions given on schematic

LIATHITE JR

Liathite Jr

This unisex hoodie is a fast and fun knit and your child will love to wear it. Knit from the top down in one piece with raglan shoulder shaping.

Sizes

To fit actual chest up to size: 20 (21, 22, 23, 25, 27, 29)" / 51 (53.5, 56, 58.5, 63.5, 68.5, 73.5) cm
Suggested Ages: 12 mts (18 mts, 2 yrs, 4 yrs, 6 yrs, 8 yrs, 10 yrs)

Finished Measurements

Chest Circumference: 21.5 (23.75, 24.75, 27.25, 28.25, 30.5, 31.75)" / 54.5 (60.5, 63, 69, 72, 77.5, 80.5) cm
Size 28.25" / 72 cm modeled on 6 yr old with approx. 3" / 7.5 cm of positive ease.
Length: 14 (15, 15.75, 18.25, 19.5, 21, 21.75)" / 35.5 (38, 40, 46.5, 49.5, 53.5, 55) cm not including hood.

Materials

Yarn
Berroco 'Vintage Chunky' (50% Acrylic, 40% Wool, 10% Nylon; 130 yds / 120 m per 3.5 oz / 100g skein); Color: Smoke (6106); 3 (4, 5, 5, 6, 7, 7) skeins.

Needles & Notions
Size 10 US / 6 mm circular needle, 32" / 80 cm length (or longer, to suit size made)
Size 9 US / 5.5 mm circular needle, 32" / 80 cm length (or longer, to suit size made) for ribbing
(Size 10 US / 6 mm & 9 US / 5.5 mm dpns, if magic loop method is not used for sleeves)
Stitch markers (including 4 split ring), cable needle, waste yarn, tapestry needle, open zip approx. 12.5 (13.5, 14, 16.5, 17.25, 18.75, 19.25)" / 32 (34.5, 35.5, 42, 44, 48, 49) cm long (or longer, can be cut to length).

Gauge

14 sts / 20 rows = 4" / 10 cm in st st with larger needle
Four Rib Braid chart meas 3" / 7.5 cm across with larger needle
18 sts / 22 rows = 4" / 10 cm in 2x2 Ribbing (*relaxed*) with smaller needle
Adjust needle size if necessary to obtain correct gauge.

Pattern Notes

See techniques section on page 48: Short Rows, Cable Cast On, Backward Loop Cast On & 3-Needle Bind Off.

Cable Chart & Instructions
2/1/2 RC Sl 3 sts on cn & hold at back of work, k2, sl final p st from cn to LH needle & p, k2 from cn.
2/1 RPC Sl 1 st on cn & hold at back of work, k2, p1 from cn.
2/1 LPC Sl 2 sts on cn & hold at front of work, p1, k2 from cn.
2/2 RC Sl 2 sts on cn & hold at back of work, k2, k2 from cn.
2/2 LC Sl 2 sts on cn & hold at front of work, k2, k2 from cn.
2/1/2 LC Sl 3 sts on cn & hold at front of work, k2, sl final p st from cn to LH needle & p, k2 from cn.

Four Rib Braid
Row 1 (WS): [K2, p2] twice, k1, [p2, k2] twice.
Row 2 (RS): P2, k2, p2, 2/1/2 RC, p2, k2, p2.
Row 3 (WS): [K2, p2] twice, k1, [p2, k2] twice.
Row 4 (RS): P2, 2/1 LPC, 2/1 RPC, p1, 2/1 LPC, 2/1 RPC, p2.
Row 5 (WS): [K3, p4] twice, k3.
Row 6 (RS): P3, 2/2 RC, p3, 2/2 LC, p3.
Row 7 (WS): [K3, p4] twice, k3.
Row 8 (RS): P2, 2/1 RPC, 2/1 LPC, p1, 2/1 RPC, 2/1 LPC, p2.
Row 9 (WS): [K2, p2] twice, k1, [p2, k2] twice.
Row 10 (RS): P2, k2, p2, 2/1/2 LC, p2, k2, p2.

Row 11 (WS): [K2, p2] twice, k1, [p2, k2] twice.
Row 12 (RS): P2, 2/1 LPC, 2/1 RPC, p1, 2/1 LPC, 2/1 RPC, p2.
Row 13 (WS): [K3, p4] twice, k3.
Row 14 (RS): P3, 2/2 RC, p3, 2/2 LC, p3.
Row 15 (WS): [K3, p4] twice, k3.
Row 16 (RS): P2, 2/1 RPC, 2/1 LPC, p1, 2/1 RPC, 2/1 LPC, p2.

PATTERN

YOKE
With larger circ needle, CO 26 (26, 26, 28, 28, 30, 30) sts.
Set-Up Row (WS): P2, pm, p4, pm, p14 (14, 14, 16, 16, 18, 18), pm, p4, pm, p2.

Sizes - (-, -, -, 6 yrs, 8 yrs, 10 yrs) only
Raglan Inc Row (RS): *Knit to last st before m, M1R, k1, sl m, k1, M1L; rep from * 3 more times, knit to end of row. - (-, -, -, 36, 38, 38) sts - *8 sts inc'd.*
Next Row (WS & all WS rows): Purl.

Sizes 12mts (18 mts, 2 yrs, 4 yrs, -, -, -)
Neck Inc Row (RS): Kf&b, *knit to last st before m, M1R, k1, sl m, k1, M1L; rep from * 3 more times, k1, kf&b. 36 (36, 36, 38, -, -, -) sts – *10 sts inc'd.*
Next Row (WS & all WS rows): Purl.
Proceed to 'All Sizes' for sizes 12mts & 18mts

Sizes - (-, 2 yrs, 4 yrs, 6 yrs, 8 yrs, 10 yrs) only
Neck Inc Row (RS): K1, M1R, *knit to last st before m, M1R, k1, sl m, k1, M1L; rep from * 3 more times, knit to last st, M1L, k1. – *10 sts inc'd.*
Work 1 WS row.
Rep these two rows - (-, 0, 0, 1, 1, 2) more times more.
36 (36, 46, 48, 56, 58, 68) sts.

All Sizes
Neck Inc Row (RS): K1, M1R, *knit to last st before m, M1R, k1, sl m, k1, M1L; rep from * 3 more times, knit to last st, M1L, k1. – *10 sts inc'd.*
Neck Inc Row (WS): P1, M1p, purl to last st, M1p, p1. – *2 sts inc'd.*
Rep these two rows once more.
60 (60, 70, 72, 80, 82, 92) sts.

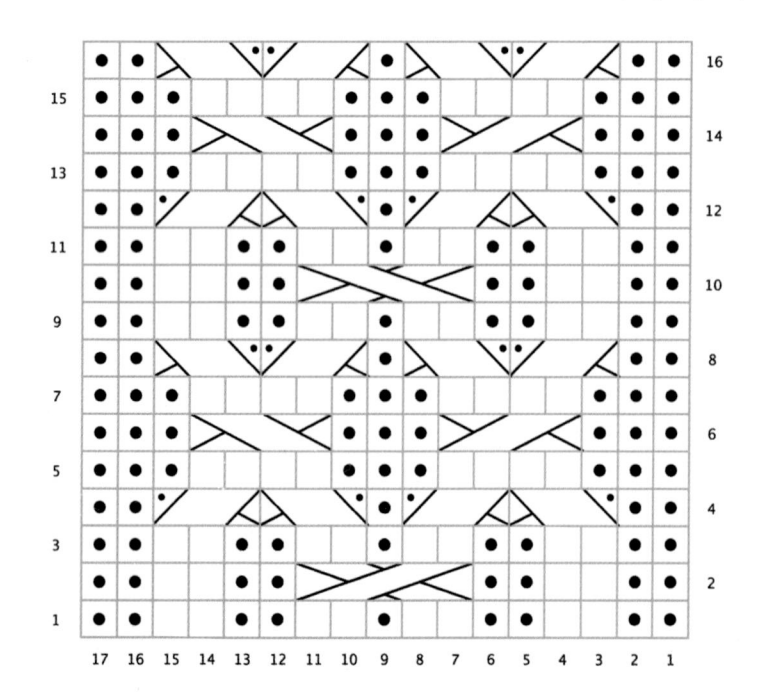

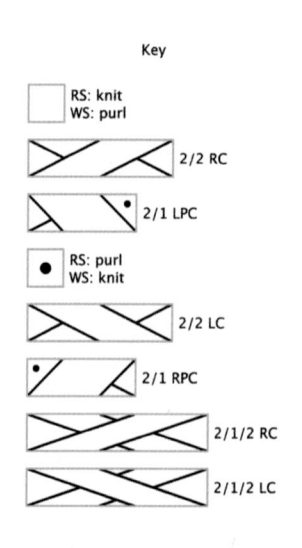

Key

- □ RS: knit / WS: purl
- 2/2 RC
- 2/1 LPC
- ● RS: purl / WS: knit
- 2/2 LC
- 2/1 RPC
- 2/1/2 RC
- 2/1/2 LC

Sizes 12 mts & 18 mts only
Neck Cast On Row (RS): Using Cable Cast On, CO 9 sts, k2, sl 1, (p2, k2) twice, p1, k2, p2, k2, *knit to last st before m, M1R, k1, sl m, k1, M1L; rep from * 3 more times, knit to end of row. 77 (77, -, -, -, -, -) sts.
Neck Cast On Row (WS): Using Cable Cast On, CO 9 sts, p3, work Four Rib Braid (omitting final st of chart), purl to last 19 sts, work Four Rib Braid (*omitting 1st st of chart*), p3. 86 (86, -, -, -, -, -) sts.
Raglan Inc Row (RS): K2, sl 1 p-wise, work Four Rib Braid over next 16 sts (*omitting final st of chart*), *knit to last st before m, M1R, k1, sl m, k1, M1L; rep from * 3 more times, work Four Rib Braid (*omitting 1st st of chart*), sl 1 p-wise, k2. 94 (94, -, -, -, -, -) sts.
Next Row (WS): P3, work complete Four Rib Braid, purl to last 20 sts, work complete Four Rib Braid, p3.

All other sizes
Neck Cast On Row (RS): Using Cable Cast On, CO - (-, 8, 9, 9, 10, 9) sts, k2, sl 1, (p2, k2) twice, p1, (k2, p2) twice, *knit to last st before m, M1R, k1, sl m, k1, M1L; rep from * 3 more times, knit to end of row. - (-, 86, 89, 97, 100, 109) sts.
Neck Cast On Row (WS): Using Cable Cast On, CO - (-, 8, 9, 9, 10, 9) sts, p3, work Four Rib Braid, purl to last 20 sts, work Four Rib Braid, p3.
86 (86, 94, 98, 106, 110, 118) sts.

All Sizes
Raglan Inc Row (RS): K2, sl 1 p-wise, work Four Rib Braid over next 17 sts, *knit to last st before m, M1R, k1, sl m, k1, M1L; rep from * 3 more times, knit to last 20 sts, work Four Rib Braid, sl 1 p-wise, k2. – 8 sts inc'd.
Next Row (WS): P3, work Four Rib Braid, purl to last 20 sts, work Four Rib Braid, p3.
Rep these two rows 6 (6, 6, 7, 7, 9, 8) more times. 150 (150, 150, 162, 170, 190, 190) sts.

Yoke for 12 mts size is now complete; proceed to 'Sleeve Divide Row'.

Sizes - (18 mts, 2 yrs, 4 yrs, 6 yrs, 8 yrs, 10 yrs) only
Body Inc Row (RS): *Work in patt to last st before m, M1R, k1, sl m, knit to m, sl m, k1, M1L; rep from * once more, work in patt to end of row. – 4 sts inc'd.
Next Row (WS): Work all sts in patt est'd.
Rep these two rows - (0, 1, 1, 1, 1, 2) more times.
- (154, 158, 170, 178, 198, 202) sts.

All Sizes
Sleeve Divide Row (RS): *Work in patt to m, remove m, sl 28 (28, 28, 30, 32, 36, 36) sleeve sts to waste yarn, remove m, using Backwards Loop Cast On, CO 0 (1, 1, 1, 1, 0, 0) sts, pm for side seam, CO 0 (1, 1, 1, 1, 0, 0) sts; rep from * once more, work in patt to end of row. 94 (102, 106, 114, 118, 126, 130) sts.

BODY
Work even in patt until body meas approx 6.5 (7, 7.5, 9, 10, 9.5, 10)" / 16.5 (18, 19, 23, 25.5, 24, 25.5) cm from underarm, ending with row 2, 8, 10 or 16 of Four Rib Braid Chart.

Waistband
Set-up Row (WS): With smaller circ needle, P3, [k2, p2] twice, k1, M1, *p2, k2; rep from * to last 12 sts, M1, k1, [p2, k2] twice, p3. 96 (104, 108, 116, 120, 128, 132) sts.
Next Row (RS): K2, sl 1 p-wise, *p2, k2; rep from * to last 5 sts, p2, sl 1, k2.
Next Row (WS): P3, *k2, p2; rep from * to last st, p1.
Work even in patt est'd until ribbing meas approx. 2.5 (2.5, 2.5, 3, 3, 4, 4)" / 6.5 (6.5, 6.5, 7.5, 7.5, 10, 10) cm. BO all sts loosely in patt.

SLEEVES
Sleeves will be knit in the round using magic loop or dpns.
With larger circ needle (or dpns), starting at center of underarm, pick up and knit 0 (1, 1, 1, 1, 0, 0) sts, k28 (28, 28, 30, 32, 36, 36) held sleeve sts, pick up and knit 0 (1, 1, 1, 1, 0, 0) sts from underarm, pm for start of rnd, join to work in the rnd. 28 (30, 30, 32, 34, 36, 36) sts.
Knit 7 (11, 12, 9, 8, 12, 14) rnds even.
Sleeve Dec Rnd: K2tog, knit to last 2 sts, ssk.

26 (28, 28, 30, 32, 34, 34) sts – 2 sts dec'd.
Work Sleeve Dec Rnd every 8th (-, -, 10th, 9th, 13th, 15th) rnd 1 (0, 0, 1, 2, 1, 1) more time(s).
24 (28, 28, 28, 28, 32, 32) sts.
Knit until sleeve meas approx. 5.5 (5.5, 6, 6.5, 8.5, 9, 10)" / 14 (14, 15, 16.5, 21.5, 23, 25.5) cm.

Cuff

With smaller circ needle, *K2, p2; rep from * to end of rnd.
Rep this rnd until Cuff meas approx. 2.5 (3, 4, 4.5, 4.5, 5, 5)" / 6.5 (7.5, 10, 11.5, 11.5, 12.5, 12.5) cm.
BO all sts in patt loosely.

Finishing

Hood

Fold front edging along slip st and pin in place on the inside of work. Note that when picking up sts for hood you will pick up 'double' sts at each edge where sts are folded down.

With RS facing and using smaller circ needle, starting at right side of cast-on neck sts, pick up and knit 6 (6, 5, 6, 6, 7, 6) sts to end of front neck cast on sts, pick up and knit 6 (6, 7, 7, 9, 9, 10) sts to edge of neck cast-on sts, pick up and knit 26 (26, 26, 28, 28, 30, 30) sts from cast-on, pick up and knit 6 (6, 7, 7, 9, 9, 10) sts to left front cast-on sts, pick up and knit final 6 (6, 5, 6, 6, 7, 6) sts. 50 (50, 50, 54, 58, 62, 62) sts.
Pm 16 (16, 16, 16, 20, 20, 20) sts from each end.

Next Row (WS): *P2, k2; rep from * to final 2 sts, p2.
Next Row (RS): *K2, p2; rep from * to final 2 sts, k2.
Work 1 WS row.
Hood Inc Row (RS): Work to m, M1, sl m, work to 2nd m, sl m, M1, work to end of row.
Note: Work M1 as knit or purl as necessary to match pattern.

Rep last four rows 7 more times. 66 (66, 66, 70, 74, 78, 78) sts.
Work even in patt until hood meas approx. 6.5 (7, 7.25, 7.75, 7.75, 8.25, 8.5)" / 16.5 (18, 18.5, 19.5, 19.5, 21, 21.5) cm ending with a WS row.
Place marker at center of sts, remove other 2 markers.

Short Row Shaping

Short Row (RS): Work in patt to 6 (6, 6, 7, 5, 5, 5) sts before m, w&t.
Next Row (WS): Work in patt to end of row.
Short Row (RS): Work in patt to 6 (6, 6, 7, 5, 5, 5) sts before previous wrapped st, w&t.
Next Row (WS): Work in patt to end of row.
Rep last two rows 2 (2, 2, 2, 4, 4, 4) more times.
Work to 1 st before m, picking up and working all wraps with st they wrap as you pass them, BO 2 sts (removing center m), work in patt to end of row.
Short Row (WS): Work in patt to 5 (5, 5, 6, 4, 4, 4) sts before BO sts, w&t.
Next Row (RS): Work in patt to end of row.
Short Row (WS): Work in patt to 6 (6, 6, 7, 5, 5, 5) sts before previous wrapped st, w&t.
Next Row (RS): Work in patt to end of row.
Rep last two rows 2 (2, 2, 2, 4, 4, 4) more times.
Turn hood inside out and bind off all sts using 3-needle bind off, taking care to pick up wraps as you pass them.

Sewing Zip in Position

With zip closed, pin each front edge to zip, bringing edges close to teeth without covering. Take care not to stretch knitting. Note that the front edges are folded under at the sl st row. If zip is longer than opening cut at top to length and fold edge down. Open zip and sew front edges of cardigan in place as close to teeth as possible.
Now working from inside, sew other edge of the zip in position. Ensure that stitches can't be seen from front of work.

Weave in loose ends using tapestry needle. Sew underarm seams if necessary. Block to dimensions given on schematic.

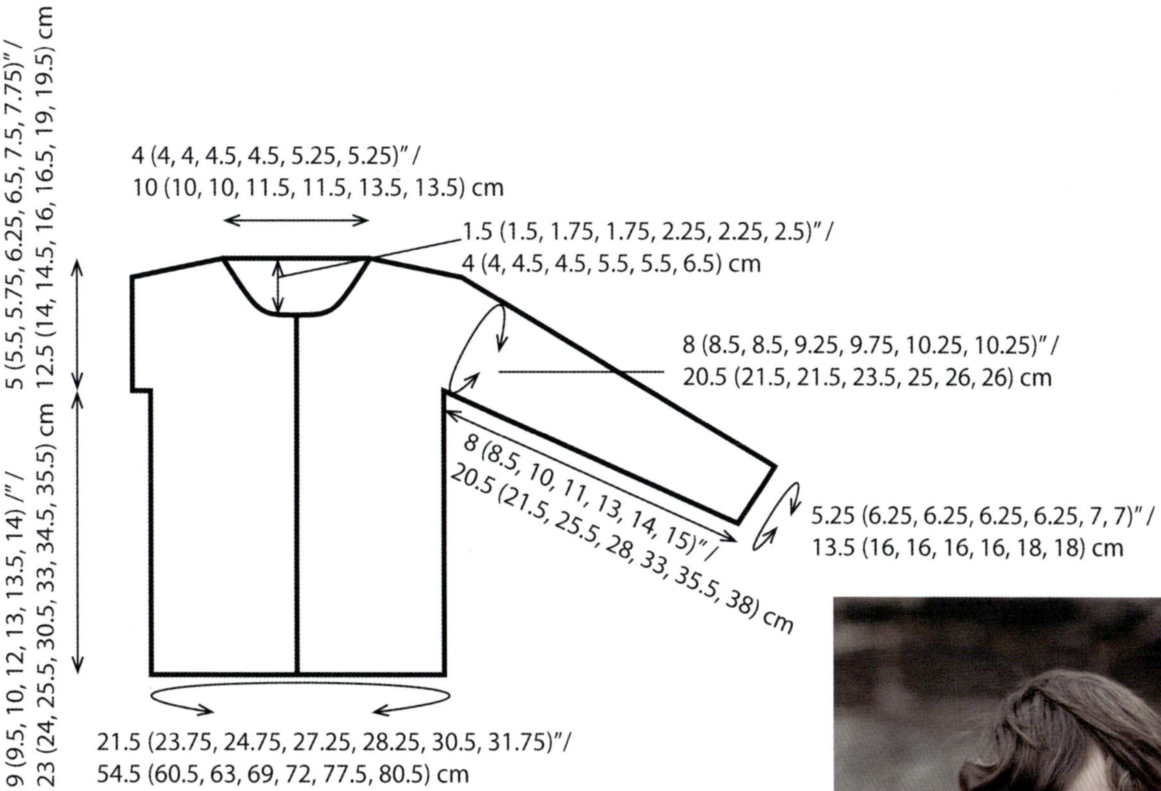

4 (4, 4, 4.5, 4.5, 5.25, 5.25)" / 10 (10, 10, 11.5, 11.5, 13.5, 13.5) cm

1.5 (1.5, 1.75, 1.75, 2.25, 2.25, 2.5)" / 4 (4, 4.5, 4.5, 5.5, 5.5, 6.5) cm

8 (8.5, 8.5, 9.25, 9.75, 10.25, 10.25)" / 20.5 (21.5, 21.5, 23.5, 25, 26, 26) cm

5 (5.5, 5.75, 6.25, 6.5, 7.5, 7.75)" / 12.5 (14, 14.5, 16, 16.5, 19, 19.5) cm

8 (8.5, 10, 11, 13, 14, 15)" / 20.5 (21.5, 25.5, 28, 33, 35.5, 38) cm

5.25 (6.25, 6.25, 6.25, 6.25, 7, 7)" / 13.5 (16, 16, 16, 16, 18, 18) cm

9 (9.5, 10, 12, 13, 13.5, 14)" / 23 (24, 25.5, 30.5, 33, 34.5, 35.5) cm

21.5 (23.75, 24.75, 27.25, 28.25, 30.5, 31.75)" / 54.5 (60.5, 63, 69, 72, 77.5, 80.5) cm

TOURMALITE

Tourmalite

Finished Measurements

Shawl Width: 47.5" / 120.5 cm
Shawl Depth: 21.5" / 54.5 cm
Dimensions after blocking.

Materials

Yarn
MC: Noro 'Silk Garden Lite' [45% Silk, 45% Kid Mohair, 10% Lamb's wool, 137 yds / 125 m per 50g]; Color: 2026; 3 skeins
CC: Cascade Yarns 'Cascade 220 Sport' [100% Wool, 164 yds / 150 m per 50g]; Color: 2452; 3 skeins

Needles & Notions
US size 8 / 5mm circular needle, 32"/ 80 cm length
US size 9 / 5.5mm needle for bind off (any needle type)
Tapestry needle, crochet hook for Provisional Cast On, waste yarn.

Gauge

18 sts / 34 rows = 4" / 10 cm in garter stitch unblocked
16 sts / 29 rows = 4" / 10 cm in garter stitch blocked

Pattern Notes

See techniques section on page 48: Short Rows in Garter (w&t), Short Rows in st st (w&t), Provisional Cast On (Crochet method) & I-cord Bind Off.

Pattern

With circ needle, and waste yarn, CO 85 sts using Provisional Cast On.
Set-up Row (WS): With MC, knit 1 row.

Short Row Wedge
*Short Row (RS): Wyif, sl 1 p-wise, knit to last 2 sts, w&t.
Next Row (WS): Knit to end of row.
Short Row (RS): Wyif, sl 1 p-wise, knit to 2 sts before previous wrapped st, w&t.
Rep these two rows 12 more times.
Work 1 more WS row.

Change to CC.
Short Row (RS): Wyif, sl 1 p-wise, knit to 2 sts before previous wrapped st, w&t.
Next Row (WS): Knit to end of row.
Rep these two rows 17 more times.

Short Row (RS): Wyif, sl 1 p-wise, knit to 2 sts before previous wrapped st, w&t.
Next Row (WS): Purl to last 3 sts, k3.
Rep these two rows 8 more times.
3 sts remain unwrapped.

Next Row (RS): Wyif, sl 1 p-wise, knit to end of row picking up and working all wraps with the st they wrap.
Next Row (WS): Purl to last 3 sts, k3.

Short Row (RS): Wyif, sl 1 p-wise, k2, w&t.
Next Row (WS): K3.
Short Row (RS): Wyif, sl 1 p-wise, knit to previous wrapped st, work wrap with st, k1, w&t.
Next Row (WS): Purl to last 3 sts, k3.
Rep these two rows 7 more times.

Short Row (RS): Wyif, sl 1 p-wise, knit to previous wrapped st, work wrap with st, k1, w&t.
Next Row (WS): Knit to end of row.
Rep these two rows 17 more times.

Change to MC.
Short Row (RS): Wyif, sl 1 p-wise, knit to previous wrapped st, work wrap with st, k1, w&t.
Next Row (WS): Knit to end of row.
Rep these two rows 13 more times.

Next Row (RS): Wyif, sl 1 p-wise, knit to end of row picking up and working remaining wrap with the st it wraps.
Next Row (WS): Purl to last 3 sts, k3.*

Rep from * to * 3 more times, omitting final WS row on the final repeat.

Edging
Working on WS, using CC and larger needles, work I-Cord Bind Off along all 85 sts, turn corner to bottom edge sts, work I-cord Bind Off along bottom edge, picking up 1 st for each slipped edge st, undo Provisional Cast On placing resulting 85 sts on circ needle, work I-cord Bind Off across all sts, turn corner to top edge, work I-cord Bind Off picking up sts as you work.
Join start and end of I-cord.

FINISHING

Weave in all loose ends. Block shawl to dimensions given.

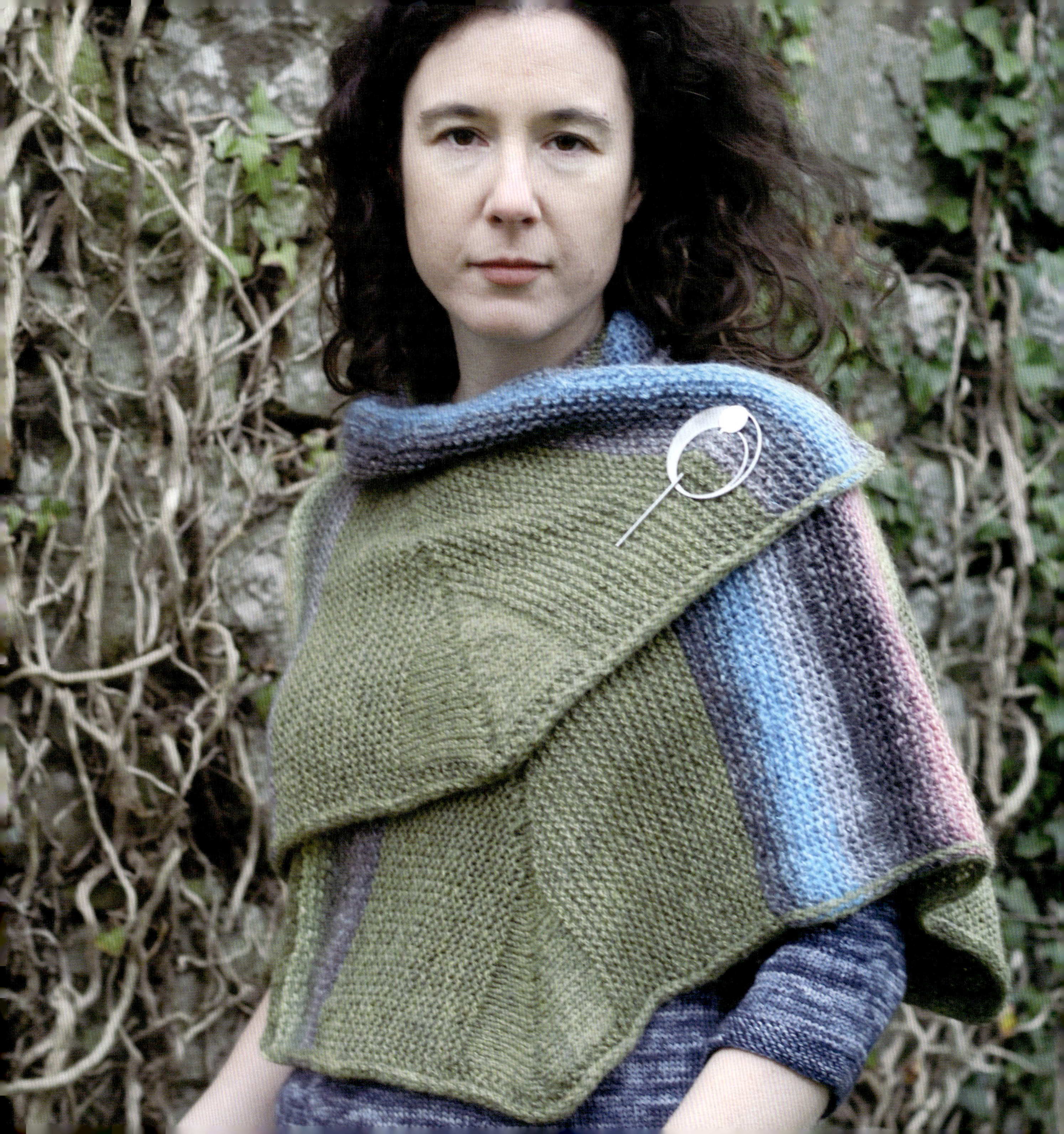

BASANITE

BASANITE

HAT SIZES

To fit head up to circumference: 22 (25)" / 56 (63.5) cm
2-3" / 5-7.5 cm negative ease recommended.

Length from crown to base: 7 (7.25)" / 18 (18.5) cm
Finished Band Circumference: 19.25 (22.5)" / 49 (57) cm

MITTEN SIZE

Hand Circumference: 7.5" / 19 cm
Wrist Circumference: 6.5" / 16.5 cm with 1" / 2.5cm flap

MATERIALS

Yarn
Hat: Quince & Co 'Puffin' (100% Wool; 112 yds / 102 m per 100g skein); Color: Birds Egg (106); 1 (1) skein.
Mittens: Quince & Co 'Puffin' (100% Wool; 112 yds / 102 m per 100g skein); Color: Birds Egg (106); 1 skein.

Needles & Notions
Size 11 US / 8mm needles
Stitch markers, tapestry needle, waste yarn, crochet hook (approx. size of needle)
Hat: 2 buttons approx. 1" / 2.5 cm diam.
Mittens: 4 buttons approx. 1" / 2.5 cm diam.

GAUGE

11 sts / 26 rows = 4" / 10 cm in garter stitch
15 sts / 30 rows = 4" / 10 cm in slipped stitch pattern stitch
Adjust needle size if necessary to obtain the correct gauge.

PATTERN NOTES

See techniques section on page 48: Provisional Cast On & Short Rows shown in techniques section.

GARTER STITCH GRAFTING
Place an equal number of stitches on the front and back needles; break yarn leaving a generous tail. Thread a tapestry needle with the yarn. Purl 'bumps' should be on side nearest you.
Grafting of hat involves only garter stitch grafting. First 3 sts of mittens begin with st st (as shown below) and the remainder is garter stitch grafting.

Mitten first 3 sts:
Step 1:
Pull needle through first front stitch as if to purl.
Step 2:
Pull needle through first back stitch as if to knit.
Step 3:
Pull needle through first front stitch as if to knit and slip stitch off needle.
Pull needle through next front stitch as if to purl but leave stitch on needle.
Step 4:
Pull needle through first back stitch as if to purl and slip stitch off needle.
Pull needle through next back stitch as if to knit but leave stitch on needle.
Rep steps 3 & 4 once, then work step 3 once more.
Step 5:
Pull needle through first back stitch as if to purl and slip stitch off needle.
Pull needle through next back stitch as if to purl but leave stitch on needle.
Work remainder of mitten grafting as steps 3 & 4 below.

Garter Stitch Grafting
Step 1:
Pull needle through first front stitch as if to purl.
Step 2:
Pull needle through first back stitch as if to purl.

Step 3:
Pull needle through first front stitch as if to knit and slip stitch off needle.
Pull needle through next front stitch as if to purl but leave stitch on needle.

Step 4:
Pull needle through first back stitch as if to knit and slip stitch off needle.
Pull needle through next back stitch as if to purl but leave stitch on needle.
Rep steps 3 and 4 until all stitches have been worked. Take care to pull yarn carefully through worked stitches periodically. Make sure you do not work it too tight; it should look like a knitted stitch.

HAT PATTERN

Using Provisional Cast On method, CO 24 (25) sts. Knit one row.
Row 1 (RS): K5, (sl 2 wyif, k2) twice, pm (sl this marker after first rep), k11 (12).
Row 2 (WS): Knit to m, sl m, p1, (sl 2 wyib, p2) twice, p1, sl 3 wyif.
Row 3 (RS): K3, sl 2 wyif, (k2, sl2 wyif) twice, sl m, k10 (11), w&t.
Row 4 (WS): Knit to m, sl m, p1, (p2, sl 2 wyib) twice, p1, sl 3 wyif.
Row 5 (RS): K5, (sl 2 wyif, k2) twice, sl m, k9 (10), w&t.
Row 6 (WS): Knit to m, sl m, p1, (sl 2 wyib, p2) twice, p1, sl 3 wyif.
Row 7 (RS): K3, sl 2 wyif, (k2, sl 2 wyif) twice, sl m, k8 (9), w&t.
Row 8 (WS): Knit to m, sl m, p1, (p2, sl 2 wyib) twice, p1, sl 3 wyif.
Row 9 (RS): K5, (sl 2 wyif, k2) twice, sl m, k7 (8), w&t.
Row 10 (WS): Knit to m, sl m, p1, (sl 2 wyib, p2) twice, p1, sl 3 wyif.
Row 11 (RS): K3, sl 2 wyif, (k2, sl 2 wyif) twice, sl m, k6 (7), w&t.
Row 12 (WS): Knit to m, sl m, p1, (p2, sl 2 wyib) twice, p1, sl 3 wyif.
Row 13 (RS): K3, sl 2 wyif, (k2, sl 2 wyif) twice, sl m, k5 (6), w&t.
Row 14 (WS): Knit to m, sl m, p1, (sl 2 wyib, p2) twice, p1, sl 3 wyif.
Row 15 (RS): K5, (sl 2 wyif, k2) twice, sl m, k4 (5), w&t.
Row 16 (WS): Knit to m, sl m, p1, (p2, sl 2 wyib) twice, p1, sl 3 wyif.
Row 17 (RS): K3, sl 2 wyif, (k2, sl 2 wyif) twice, sl m, k3 (4), w&t.
Row 18 (WS): Knit to m, sl m, p1, (sl 2 wyib, p2) twice, p1, sl 3 wyif.
Row 19 (RS): K5, (sl 2 wyif, k2) twice, sl m, k2 (3), w&t.
Row 20 (WS): Knit to m, sl m, p1, (p2, sl 2 wyib) twice, p1, sl 3 wyif.
Row 21 (RS): K3, sl 2 wyif, (k2, sl 2 wyif) twice, sl m, k1 (2), w&t.
Row 22 (WS): Knit to m, sl m, p1, (sl 2 wyib, p2) twice, p1, sl 3 wyif.
Row 23 (RS): K5, (sl 2 wyif, k2) twice, sl m, k0 (1), w&t.
Row 24 (WS): K0 (1), sl m, p1, (p2, sl 2 wyib) twice, p1, sl 3 wyif.
Rep these twenty-four rows 5 (6) more times, on Row 1 picking up all wraps as you pass them and working them with the st they wrap.
Work Row 1 once more.

Undo Provisional Cast On and place all sts on needle. With WS facing, graft first 11 (12) sts of row to corresponding sts picked up from cast on using garter stitch grafting method. BO remaining 13 sts from cast on edge, leaving 13 sts from end of piece on needle. Rejoin yarn on WS to remaining 13 sts. We will continue hat edge to form flap.
Row 1 (WS): P1, (sl 2 wyib, p2) twice, p1, sl 3 wyif.
Row 2 (RS): K3, sl 2 wyif, (k2, sl 2 wyif) twice.
Row 3 (WS): P1, (p2, sl 2 wyib) twice, p1, sl 3 wyif.
Row 4 (RS): K5, (sl 2 wyif, k2) twice.
Rep Rows 1-4 once more, then rep Rows 1-3 once more.

Bind Off Row (RS): *K2, sl 1, k1, psso, sl 3 sts from RH to LH needle p-wise; rep from * until 3 sts remain on RH needle, sl sts to LH needle, k3.
Turn work 90 degrees to pick up sts along top of flap.
*Sl 3 sts from RH to LH needle, k2, sl 1, pick up & knit 1 st from edge of flap, psso; rep from * until I-cord

edging is worked to end of flap, k3tog, break yarn & draw through final st.

FINISHING

Weave in all loose ends. Sew flap in position. Sew button to flap. Block hat, taking care to shape well, possibly by blocking around a bowl.

MITTEN PATTERN

Note on Sizing: These mittens are written in one size only due to the large gauge of the yarn and long pattern repeat. However if you want to work for a slightly larger hand, just work a few more short rows at the thumb and add a stitch or two to the length of the garter stitch body.

LEFT MITTEN

Using Provisional Cast On method, CO 28 sts. Knit one row.
Row 1 (RS): K5, (sl 2 wyif, k2) twice, pm (sl after first rep), knit to last 3 sts, sl 3 wyif.
*Row 2 (WS): Knit to m, sl m, p1, (sl 2 wyib, p2) twice, p1, sl 3 wyif.
Row 3 (RS): K3, sl 2 wyif, (k2, sl 2 wyif) twice, sl m, knit to last 3 sts, sl 3 wyif.
Row 4 (WS): Knit to m, sl m, p1, (p2, sl 2 wyib) twice, p1, sl 3 wyif.

Rep Rows 1-4 twice more.

Row 13 (RS): K3, sl 2 wyif, (k2, sl 2 wyif) twice, sl m, knit to last 3 sts, sl 3 wyif.
Row 14 (WS): Knit to m, sl m, p1, (sl 2 wyib, p2) twice, p1, sl 3 wyif.
Row 15 (RS): K5, (sl 2 wyif, k2) twice, sl m, knit to last 3 sts, sl 3 wyif.
Row 16 (WS): Knit to m, sl m, p1, (p2, sl 2 wyib) twice, p1, sl 3 wyif.

Rep Rows 13-16 twice more.* 24 rows worked in total.

Thumb Gusset
Row 1 (RS): K5, (sl 2 wyif, k2) twice, sl m, k6, place rem 9 sts on holder. Turn.
Short Row 1 (WS): Using Cable Cast On, CO 2 sts, k7, w&t.
Next Row (RS & all RS): Knit to last 2 sts, sl 2 wyif.
Short Row 2 (WS): K6, w&t.
Short Row 3 (WS): K5, w&t.
Short Row 4 (WS): K4, w&t.
Short Row 5 (WS): K3, w&t.
Next Row (RS): K3tog, place 9 held sts on LH needle and knit to last 3 sts, sl 3 wyif.

Note: On next row when you pass wrap, work with st it wraps.
Work Rows 2-24 once more (from * to *).
Work Row 1 once more.
Undo Provisional Cast On and place all sts on needle. With WS facing, graft first 15 sts of row to corresponding sts picked up from cast on using garter stitch grafting method. BO remaining 13 sts from cast on edge, leaving 13 sts from end of piece on needle.

Rejoin yarn on WS of remaining 13 sts. We will continue mitten edge to form flap.
Row 1 (WS): P1, (sl 2 wyib, p2) twice, p1, sl 3 wyif.
Row 2 (RS): K3, sl 2 wyif, (k2, sl 2 wyif) twice.
Row 3 (WS): P1, (p2, sl 2 wyib) twice, p1, sl 3 wyif.
Row 4 (RS): K5, (sl 2 wyif, k2) twice.
Rep Rows 1 – 3 once more.

Bind Off Row (RS): *K2, sl 1, k1, psso, sl 3 sts from RH to LH needle p-wise; rep from * until 3 sts remain on RH needle, sl to LH needle, k3.
Turn work 90 degrees to pick up sts along top of flap as follows: *Sl 3 sts from RH to LH needle, k2, sl 1, pick up & knit 1 st from edge of flap, psso; rep from * until I-cord edging is worked to end of flap, k3tog, break yarn & draw through final st.

Right Mitten

Using Provisional Cast On method, CO 28 sts. Knit one row.
Row 1 (RS): K15, pm (sl after first rep), k2, (sl 2 wyif, k2) twice, sl 3 wyif.
*Row 2 (WS): K3, p1, (sl 2 wyib, p2) twice, p1, sl m, knit to last 3 sts, sl 3 wyif.
Row 3 (RS): Knit to m, sl m, sl 2 wyif, (k2, sl 2 wyif) twice, sl 3 wyif.
Row 4 (WS): K3, p1, (p2, sl 2 wyib) twice, p1, sl m, knit to last 3 sts, sl 3 wyif.

Rep Rows 1-4 twice more.

Row 13 (RS): Knit to m, sl m, sl 2 wyif, (k2, sl 2 wyif) twice, sl 3 wyif.
Row 14 (WS): K3, p1, (sl 2 wyib, p2) twice, p1, sl m, knit to last 3 sts, sl 3 wyif.
Row 15 (RS): Knit to m, sl m, k2, (sl 2 wyif, k2) twice, sl 3 wyif.
Row 16 (WS): K3, p1, (p2, sl 2 wyib) twice, p1, sl m, knit to last 3 sts, sl 3 wyif.

Rep Rows 13- 16 twice more.* 24 rows worked in total.

Thumb Gusset
Row 1 (RS): K9, put these 9 sts on holder, using Cable Cast On, CO 2 sts, k7, w&t.
Next Row (WS & all WS): Knit to last 2 sts, sl 2 wyif.
Short Row 2 (RS): K6, w&t.
Short Row 3 (RS): K5, w&t.
Short Row 4 (RS): K4, w&t.
Short Row 5 (RS): K3, w&t.
Next Row (RS): K3tog, knit to m picking up all wraps and working with st they wrap as you pass, k2, (sl 2 wyif, k2) twice, sl 3 wyif.
Place held sts back on needle. Complete rows are worked again.
Work Rows 2-24 once more (from * to *).
Undo Provisional Cast On and place all sts on needle. With RS facing, graft first 15 sts of row to corresponding sts picked up from cast on using garter stitch grafting method. BO remaining 13 sts from cast on edge, leaving 13 sts from end of piece on needle. Rejoin yarn on RS of remaining 13 sts. We will continue mitten edge to form flap.
Row 1 (RS): K2, (sl 2 wyif, k2) twice, sl 3 wyif.
Row 2 (WS): K3, p1, (sl 2 wyib, p2) twice, p1.
Row 3 (RS): Sl 2 wyif, (k2, sl 2 wyif) twice, sl 3 wyif.
Row 4 (WS): K3, p1, (p2, sl 2 wyib) twice, p1.
Rep Rows 1–3 once more.

Bind Off Row (WS): *K2, sl 1, k1, psso, sl 3 sts from RH to LH needle p-wise; rep from * until 3 sts remain on RH needle, sl to LH needle, k3.
Turn work 90 degrees to pick up sts along top of flap as follows: *Sl 3 sts from RH to LH needle, k2, sl 1, pick up & knit 1 st from edge of flap, psso; rep from * until I-cord edging is worked to end of flap, k3tog, break yarn & draw through final st.

Finishing

Weave in all loose ends. Sew flaps in position. Sew buttons to flap. Block mittens gently to dimensions given.

31

Gabbro

Gabbro

Lightweight and elegant, the delicate lace and short row hem details add a unique touch to this special garment. Worked from the top down in one piece with raglan shoulder shaping. Delicate hem details are worked using short rows.

Size

To fit actual bust circumference up to: 31.25 (34, 37, 40.25, 43, 46, 49.25, 52.5)" / 79.5 (86.5, 94, 102, 109, 117, 125, 133.5) cm.

Finished Measurements

Bust Circumference: 31.25 (34, 37, 40.25, 43, 46, 49.25, 52.5)" / 79.5 (86.5, 94, 102, 109, 117, 125, 133.5) cm.
Length: 26.75 (27, 27.75, 28.25, 29, 29.25, 29.75, 30)" / 68 (68.5, 70.5, 72, 73.5, 74.5, 75.5, 76) cm to longest point of short row hem.
Size 34" / 86.5cm modeled with no ease.

Materials

Yarn
Coolree 'Merino/Silk' (50% Merino, 50% Silk, 400 m / 437 yds per 100g); Color: Gale Force Grey: 3 (3, 3, 3, 4, 4, 4, 5) skeins.

Needles & Notions
1 US size 4 / 3.5mm circular needle, 32" / 80 cm long (*or longer for bigger sizes*)
1 set US size 4 / 3.5mm double-point needles (*if magic loop is not used for sleeves*)

Always use a needle size that gives you the gauge listed, as every knitter's gauge is unique.

Stitch markers; waste yarn; tapestry needle.

Gauge

25 sts / 32 rows = 4" / 10 cm in st st

Pattern Notes

See techniques section on page 48: Backwards loop cast on, Short Rows, Elastic Bind off, Garter stitch flat & Garter stitch in the round.

Front Panel Chart

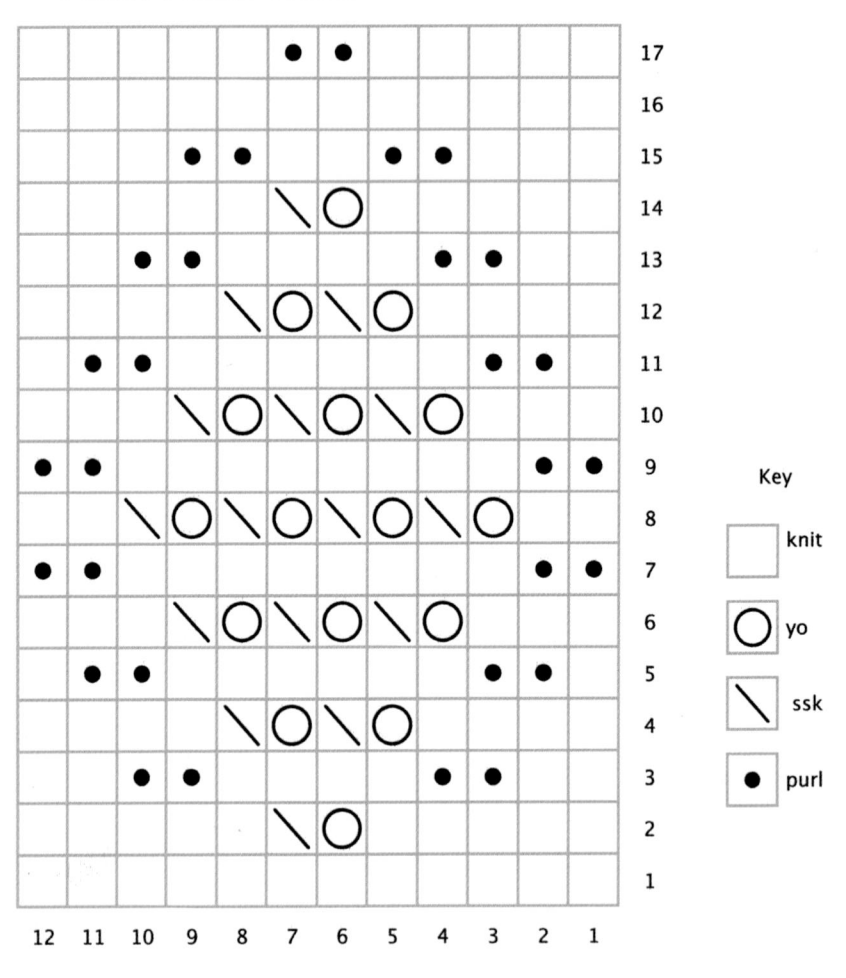

Front Panel

Rnd 1: K12.
Rnd 2: K5, yo, ssk, k5.
Rnd 3: K2, p2, k4, p2, k2.
Rnd 4: K4, (yo, ssk) twice, k4.
Rnd 5: K1, p2, k6, p2, k1.
Rnd 6: K3, (yo, ssk) three times, k3.
Rnd 7: P2, k8, p2.
Rnd 8: K2, (yo, ssk) four times, k2.
Rnd 9: P2, k8, p2.
Rnd 10: K3, (yo, ssk) three times, k3.
Rnd 11: K1, p2, k6, p2, k1.
Rnd 12: K4, (yo, ssk) twice, k4.
Rnd 13: K2, p2, k4, p2, k2.
Rnd 14: K5, yo, ssk, k5.
Rnd 15: K3, p2, k2, p2, k3.
Rnd 16: K12.
Rnd 17: K5, p2, k5

Key
☐ knit
◯ yo
╲ ssk
● purl

Side Panel

Multiple of 10 sts plus 8

Rnd 1 & all odd rnds: Knit
Rnd 2: K2, (k2tog, yo) twice, *k3, yo, ssk, k1, (k2tog, yo) twice; rep from * to last 2 sts, k2.
Rnd 4: K3, k2tog, yo, k1, *k2, (yo, ssk) twice, k1, k2tog, yo, k1; rep from * to last 2 sts, k2.
Rnd 6: K6, *k1, (yo, ssk) three times, k3; rep from * to last 2 sts, k2.
Rnd 8: K6, *(yo, ssk) four times, k2; rep from * to last 2 sts, k2.
Rnd 10: K6, *k1, (yo, ssk) three times, k3; rep from * to last 2 sts, k2.
Rnd 12: K3, k2tog, yo, k1, *k2, (yo, ssk) twice, k1, k2tog, yo, k1; rep from * to last 2 sts, k2.
Rnd 14: K2, (k2tog, yo) twice, *k3, yo, ssk, k1, (k2tog, yo) twice; rep from * to last 2 sts, k2.
Rnd 16: K1, (k2tog, yo) three times, *k4, (k2tog, yo) three times; rep from * to last st, k1.
Rnd 18: (K2tog, yo) four times, *k2, (k2tog, yo) four times; rep from * to end of rnd.
Rnd 20: K1, (k2tog, yo) three times, k1, *k3, (k2tog, yo) three times, k1; rep from * to end of rnd.

Side Panel Chart

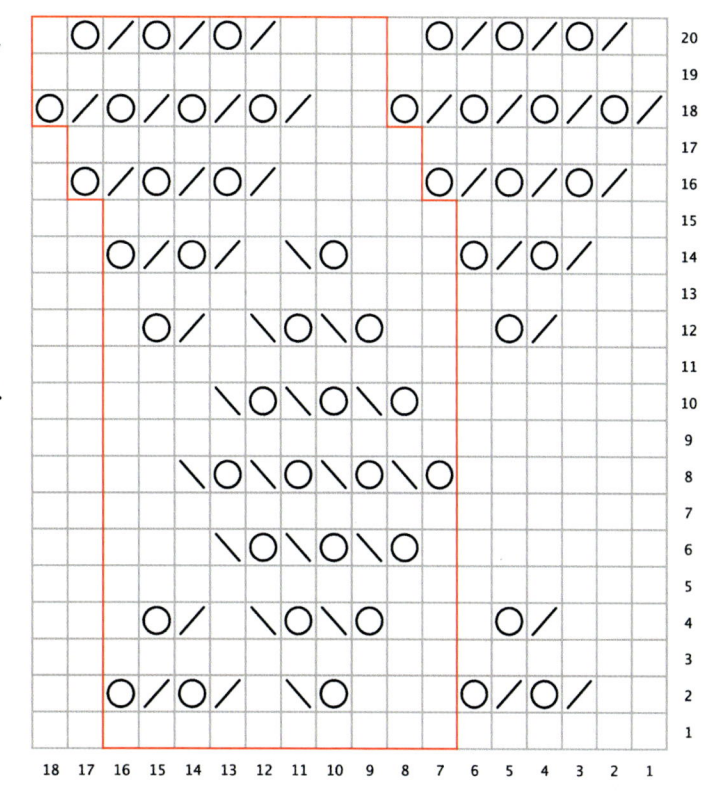

Key
- knit
- O yo
- \ ssk
- / k2tog
- Pattern Repeat

PATTERN

Note until neckline is joined first st of every row is sl k-wise wyif.

With circ needle, CO 62 (54, 56, 56, 58, 60, 62, 64) sts. Work 6 rows in garter st (sl first st of each row k-wise wyif).

Short Row 1 (RS): K43 (39, 41, 41, 43, 45, 47, 49) sts, w&t.

Short Row 2 (WS): P24 (24, 26, 26, 28, 30, 32, 34) sts, w&t.

Short Row 3: Work in st st to wrapped st, work wrap with st it wraps, work 1 more st, w&t.
Rep this row 3 more times.
Knit to end of RS row, picking up any wrap you pass.

Next Row (WS): K3, purl to last 3 sts picking up any wrap you pass, k3.

Set-Up Row (RS): K3, M1R, k1, pm, k1, M1L, k6 (2, 2, 2, 2, 2, 2, 2), M1R, k1, pm, k1, M1L, k36 (36, 38, 38, 40, 42, 44, 46), M1R, k1, pm, k1, M1L, k6 (2, 2, 2, 2, 2, 2, 2), M1R, k1, pm, k1, M1L, k3. 70 (62, 64, 64, 66, 68, 70, 72) sts – *8 sts inc'd.*

Next Row (WS): K3, purl to last 3 sts, k3.

Inc Row (RS): K3, M1R, *knit to 1 st before m, M1R, k1, sl m, k1, M1L; rep from * 3 more times, knit to last 3 sts, M1L, k3. 80 (72, 74, 74, 76, 78, 80, 82) sts – *10 sts inc'd.*
Rep these two rows 14 (14, 15, 15, 16, 17, 18, 19) more times. Do not turn at end of last row. 220 (212, 224, 224, 236, 248, 260, 272) sts.

Joining Rnd (RS): Join to work in rnd, k6, pm for start of rnd, knit to 12 sts before end of rnd, pm (lace m), work Front Panel Chart.

Raglan Inc Rnd 1: *Knit to 1 st before m, M1R, k1, sl m, k1, M1L; rep from * 3 more times, knit to lace m, work Front Panel Chart. 228 (220, 232, 232, 244, 256, 268, 280) sts – *8 sts inc'd.*

Next Rnd: Knit to lace m, sl m, work Front Panel Chart.
Rep these two rnds 7 more times, Front Panel Chart is now complete, remove lace m. 284 (276, 288, 288, 300, 312, 324, 336) sts.

Raglan Inc Rnd 2: *Knit to 1 st before m, M1R, k1, sl m, k1, M1L; rep from * 3 more times, knit to end of rnd. 292 (284, 296, 296, 308, 320, 332, 344) sts – *8 sts inc'd.*

Next Rnd: Knit to end of rnd.
Rep these two rnds 3 (4, 4, 4, 4, 4, 4, 5) more times. 316 (316, 328, 328, 340, 352, 364, 384) sts.

31.25 & 34" / 79.5 & 86.5cm are now complete; proceed to Sleeve Divide Rnd.

Sizes 37, 40.25, 43, 46, 49.25 & 52.5" / 94, 102, 109, 117, 125 & 133.5 cm only

Body Inc Rnd: *Knit to 1 st before m, M1R, k1, sl m, knit to next m, sl m, k1, M1L; rep from * once more, knit to end of rnd.
- (-, 332, 332, 344, 356, 368, 388) sts – *4 sts inc'd.*

Next Rnd: Knit to end of rnd.
Rep these two rnds - (-, 1, 3, 3, 4, 5, 6) more times.
- (-, 336, 344, 356, 372, 388, 412) sts; 94 (96, 104, 108, 112, 118, 124, 132) front/back sts, 64 (62, 64, 64, 66, 68, 70, 74) sleeves sts.

All Sizes

Sleeve Divide Rnd: *Knit to m, remove m, sl next 64 (62, 64, 64, 66, 68, 70, 74) sleeves sts onto waste yarn, remove 2nd m, CO 2 (5, 6, 9, 11, 13, 15, 16) sts using Backwards Loop method, pm for new start of rnd, CO 2 (5, 6, 9, 11, 13, 15, 16) sts; rep from * once more (2nd m will be side seam m), knit to new end of rnd, removing old start of rnd m.
196 (212, 232, 252, 268, 288, 308, 328) sts.

Next Rnd: Knit to 9 sts before side seam m, place Side Panel m, work Side Panel Chart (remove side seam m) over next 18 sts, pm, knit to end of rnd.
Cont in patt, working Side Panel Chart between Side Panel markers and rest of rnd in st st, for 13 more rnds.

Dart Placement Rnd: Work in patt for 33 (35, 39, 42, 45, 48, 51, 55) sts, pm for dart (dm), work 32 (36, 38, 42, 44, 48, 52, 54) sts in patt, pm, work 66 (70, 78, 84, 90, 96, 102, 110) sts in patt, pm, work 32 (36, 38, 42, 44, 48, 52, 54) sts, pm, work to end of rnd.

Waist Dec Rnd: *Work to 2 sts before dm, k2tog, sl m, work to next dm, sl m, ssk; rep from * once, work to end of rnd.
192 (208, 228, 248, 264, 284, 304, 324) sts – *4 sts dec'd.*
Rep Waist Dec Rnd every 8 (8, 7, 7, 7, 7, 6, 6)th rnd 4 (4,

2, 2, 2, 4, 2, 6) times & then every 9 (9, 8, 8, 8, 8, 7, -)th rnd 2 (2, 4, 4, 4, 2, 4, -) times.
168 (184, 204, 224, 240, 260, 280, 300) sts.
Work even in patt for 12 rnds. Work should now meas approx. 10 (10, 9.5, 9.5, 9.5, 9.25, 8.75, 8.25)" / 25.5 (25.5, 24, 24, 24, 23.5, 22, 21) cm from underarm.
Hip Inc Rnd: *Work to dm, M1R, sl m, work to next dm, sl m, M1L; rep from * once more, work to end of rnd.
172 (188, 208, 228, 244, 264, 284, 304) sts – *4 sts inc'd*.
Rep Hip Inc Rnd every 5th rnd five times & then every 6th rnd once. 196 (212, 232, 252, 268, 288, 308, 328) sts.
Work 1 rnd even in patt, moving markers at each side of Side Panel out 10 (10, 10, 10, 10, 10, 20, 20) sts each side. Panel will now be 38 (38, 38, 38, 38, 38, 58, 58) sts. Work all sts within panel using Side Panel Chart, cont from next row to be worked.
Next Side Panel Chart row to be worked should be even number, if not work one more rnd before starting Short Row Hem.

Short Row Hem
Right Hip
Short Rows 1 & 2: Work in patt to 30 (34, 39, 44, 48, 53, 48, 53) sts past Side Panel, w&t.
*****Short Row 3:** Work in patt to 3 sts before prev wrapped st, w&t.
Rep Short Row 3, 3 (9, 11, 19, 19, 27, 15, 23) more times.
Short Row 4: Work in patt to 2 sts before prev wrapped st, w&t.
Rep Short Row 4, 15 (11, 13, 7, 11, 5, 15, 9) more times.
Short Row 5: Work in patt to 1 st before prev wrapped st, w&t.
Rep Short Row 5, 15 (13, 13, 11, 11, 9, 15, 13) more times.*

Front
Next Row (RS): K54 (60, 68, 75, 81, 89, 86, 94) sts past Side Panel, w&t.
****Next Row (WS):** K48 (52, 58, 62, 66, 72, 76, 82) sts, w&t.
Short Row: Knit to 2 sts before prev wrapped st, w&t.
Rep this Short Row 17 (19, 19, 21, 21, 23, 25, 27) times.**

Left Hip
Short Row 1: Knit to 49 (53, 58, 63, 67, 72, 77, 82) sts past start of rnd m, w&t.
Short Row 2: P98 (106, 116, 126, 134, 144, 154, 164), w&t.
Rep from * to * as for Right Hip.

Back
Next Row (RS): K73 (79, 87, 94, 100, 108, 115, 123) sts past start of rnd, w&t.
Work from ** to ** as for Front.
Side Panel Chart is now complete. Knit to end of rnd picking up and working any wraps you pass with the st they wrap.

Next Rnd: Purl
Next Rnd: Knit.
Rep these 2 rnds once more. BO all sts p-wise using Elastic Bind Off (or another stretchy bind off).

Sleeves
Sleeves will be knit in the round using magic loop or dpns.
With circ needle (or dpns), starting at center of underarm cast on sts, pick up and knit 2 (5, 6, 9, 11, 13, 15, 16) sts, k64 (62, 64, 64, 66, 68, 70, 74) held sleeve sts, pick up and knit 2 (5, 6, 9, 11, 13, 15, 16) sts from underarm, pm for start of rnd, join to work in the rnd.
68 (72, 76, 82, 88, 94, 100, 106) sts.
Work in st st for 17 (12, 11, 8, 7, 6, 6, 6) rnds.
Sleeve Dec Rnd: K2tog, knit to last 2 sts, ssk.
66 (70, 74, 80, 86, 92, 98, 104) sts - *2 sts dec'd*.
Work Sleeve Dec Rnd every 18 (13, 12, 9, 8, 7, 7, 7)th rnd 2 (3, 3, 3, 10, 11, 9, 3) more times & then every 17 (12, 11, 8, -, 6, 6, 6)th rnd 1 (2, 3, 6, -, 1, 4, 11) time(s).
60 (60, 62, 62, 66, 68, 72, 76) sts.
Work even in st st until sleeve meas approx 11 (11, 11.5, 11.5, 12, 12, 12.5, 12.5)" / 28 (28, 29, 29, 30.5, 30.5, 32, 32) cm or desired length from underarm.

Work in garter stitch for 1" / 2.5 cm ending with a purl rnd.
Next Rnd: K15 (15, 16, 16, 17, 17, 18, 19) sts, w&t.
Next Row (WS): K30 (30, 32, 32, 34, 34, 36, 38), w&t.
Short Row: Work to 2 sts before prev wrapped st, w&t.
Rep Short Row 11 (11, 13, 13, 13, 13, 13, 15) times.
Knit to end of rnd picking up all wraps as you pass them.
BO all sts p-wise.

Finishing

Weave in all ends using tapestry needle. Block garment to dimensions given on schematic.

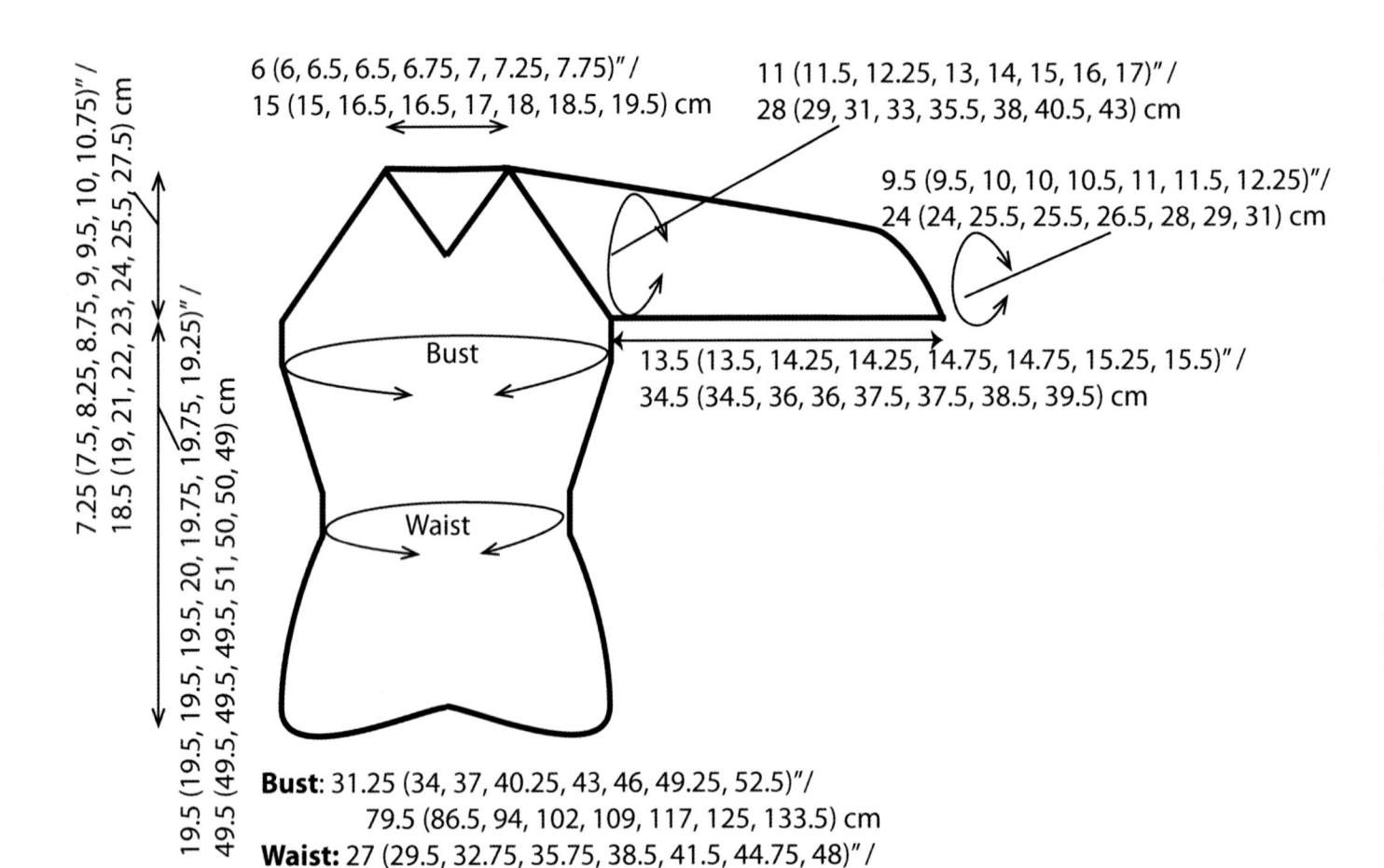

6 (6, 6.5, 6.5, 6.75, 7, 7.25, 7.75)" /
15 (15, 16.5, 16.5, 17, 18, 18.5, 19.5) cm

11 (11.5, 12.25, 13, 14, 15, 16, 17)" /
28 (29, 31, 33, 35.5, 38, 40.5, 43) cm

9.5 (9.5, 10, 10, 10.5, 11, 11.5, 12.25)" /
24 (24, 25.5, 25.5, 26.5, 28, 29, 31) cm

13.5 (13.5, 14.25, 14.25, 14.75, 14.75, 15.25, 15.5)" /
34.5 (34.5, 36, 36, 37.5, 37.5, 38.5, 39.5) cm

7.25 (7.5, 8.25, 8.75, 9, 9.5, 10, 10.75)" /
18.5 (19, 21, 22, 23, 24, 25.5, 27.5) cm

19.5 (19.5, 19.5, 20, 19.75, 19.75, 19.25)" /
49.5 (49.5, 49.5, 51, 50, 50, 49) cm

Bust: 31.25 (34, 37, 40.25, 43, 46, 49.25, 52.5)" /
79.5 (86.5, 94, 102, 109, 117, 125, 133.5) cm
Waist: 27 (29.5, 32.75, 35.75, 38.5, 41.5, 44.75, 48)" /
68.5 (75, 83, 91, 98, 105.5, 113.5, 122) cm

39

SERPENTINITE

Serpentinite

This scarf is for all the knitters out there who love scarves but hate trying to keep them on! This delicate lace scarf has an integrated beaded loop that is perfect to hold your scarf in place and creates a stunning decorative finish.

Finished Measurements

Scarf Width: 9.75" / 25 cm.
Length each side from beaded loop: 35.5" / 90 cm
Dimensions after blocking

Materials

Yarn
Hand Maiden 'Maiden Hair' (67% Silk, 23% Kid, 10% Nylon, 300 m / 328 yds per 100g); Color: Nova Scotia: 1 skein.

Needles & Notions
US size 8 / 5mm needles
US size 4 / 3.5mm needles for beaded loop
1 US size 4 / 3.5mm dpn
Always use a needle size that gives you the gauge listed, as every knitter's gauge is unique.

Tapestry needle, removable stitch marker, 194 size 6 seed beads (in sample Debbie Abrahams Beads used, 82 color 1 beads (color 606) & 112 color 2 beads (color 43)), needle & thread for threading beads.

Gauge

14 sts / 20 rows = 4" / 10 cm in lace pattern after blocking

Pattern Notes

See techniques section on page 48: Beaded Cast On, Elastic Beaded Bind Off & Threading Beads onto yarn.

See Chart on next page.

Placing Beads
To place a bead (p1b: place 1 bead, p2b: place 2 beads), work to the position you want your bead, slide your pre-strung bead(s) up your yarn until it is sitting directly behind the stitch on your right needle. Hold bead(s) in position when next stitch is being worked; the bead(s) will remain between the stitches.

42

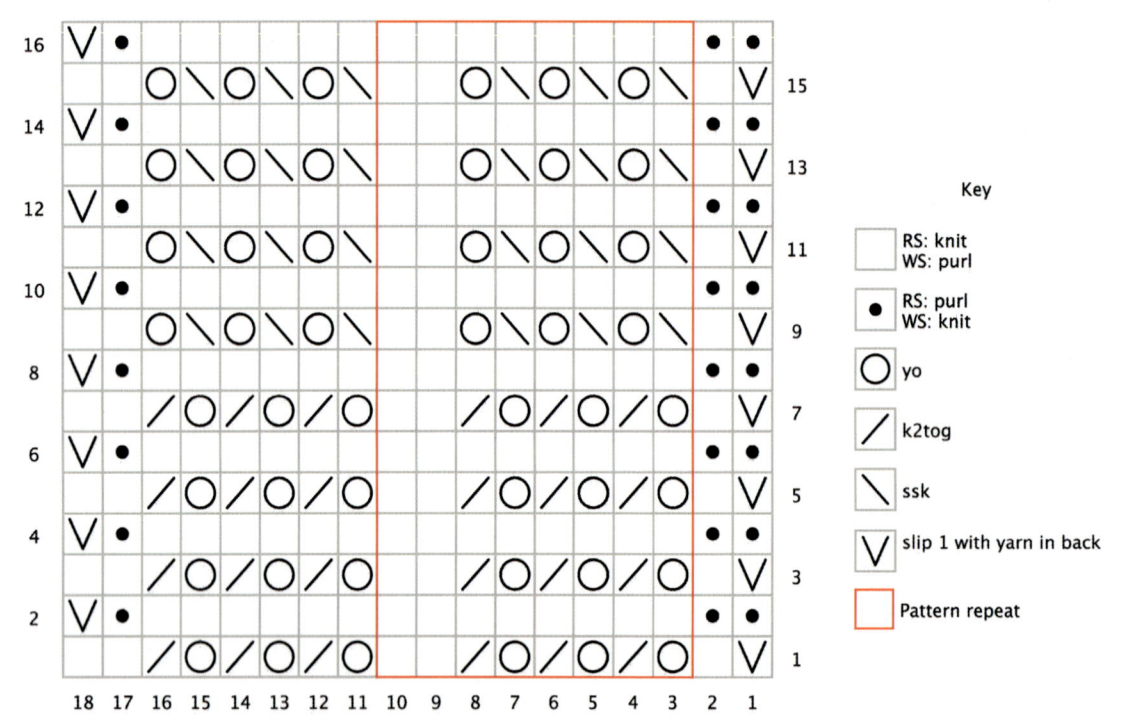

Key

- ☐ RS: knit / WS: purl
- ● RS: purl / WS: knit
- ◯ yo
- ╱ k2tog
- ╲ ssk
- V slip 1 with yarn in back
- ▢ Pattern repeat

PATTERN

If pre-stringing all beads, string 16 color 1, 56 color 2, 50 color 1, 56 color 2 & 16 color 1 for a total of 194 beads. Alternatively, thread the first 16 beads of color 1, saving the remainder to thread later.

With larger needle, CO 34 sts using beaded cast on with color 1 beads.
Knit 6 rows, sl 1st st of each row k-wise wyib.
Next Row (WS): Sl 1 k-wise wyib, k1, purl to last 2 sts, k2.

Lace Pattern
Work Rows 1-16 of chart eleven times total, or follow written instructions below, repeating Rows 1-16 eleven times total:

Rows 1, 3, 5 & 7 (RS): Sl 1 k-wise wyib, k1, *(yo, k2tog) 3 times, k2; rep from * 3 more times.
Rows 2, 4, 6, 8, 10, 12, 14 & 16 (WS): Sl 1 k-wise wyib, k1, purl to last 2 sts, k2.
Rows 9, 11, 13 & 15 (RS): Sl 1 k-wise wyib, k1, *(ssk, yo) 3 times, k2; rep from * 3 more times.

Beaded Loop
If you have not pre-strung all beads, break yarn, thread 56 color 2 beads, 50 color 1 beads & 56 color 2 beads, and rejoin yarn.

Dec Row 1 (RS): With smaller needles, sl 1 k-wise wyib, (k2tog) 16 times, k1. 18 sts.
Dec Row 2 (WS): K3tog, (k2tog) 6 times, k3tog. 8 sts.
Knit 2 rows, slipping 1st st of each row k-wise wyib and placing a removable marker or safety pin in the first row.
Beaded Row 1: Sl1, k1, p1b (color 2), k2, p2b (color 2), k2, p1b (color 2), k2. 4 beads placed in total.
Rep Beaded Row 1, 13 more times.
Beaded Row 2: Sl1, k1, p2b (color 1), k2, p1b (color 1), k2, p2b (color 1), k2. 5 beads placed in total.
Rep Beaded Row 2, 9 more times.
Rep Beaded Row 1, 14 times.
Knit 2 rows, slipping 1st st of each row k-wise wyib.
Joining Row (RS): With dpn, pick up 8 purl 'bumps' from the marked row at back (WS) of work. Hold dpn at back of work parallel to working needle. *Using 1 st from front needle and 1 st from back needle, k2tog; rep from * to end row.
Inc Row 1 (WS): (Kfb) 8 times. 16 sts.
Inc Row 2 (RS): (Kfb) 16 times. 32 sts.
Inc Row 3 (WS): With larger needle, sl 1 k-wise, k1, pfb, purl to last 3 sts, pfb, k2. 34 sts.
Rep Rows 1-16 of Lace Pattern 11 times.
Knit 6 rows, slipping 1st st of each row k-wise.
BO all sts using Elastic Beaded Bind Off with bead color 1.

FINISHING

Weave in all loose ends. Block scarf to dimensions given, taking care to open out lace.

Dolmite

Dolmite

Light as air, yet warm and cosy, this sweater is a dream to wear. A slouchy funnel neck moves into raglan shoulder shaping and the sweater finishes with a decorative flair at the hips for a relaxed fit.

SIZE

To fit actual bust circumference up to: 32.5 (35.25, 37.75, 41.75, 44.5, 47.25, 51.25, 53.75)"/ 82.5 (89.5, 95.5, 106, 113, 120, 130.5, 136.5) cm.
0-1" / 0-2.5 cm suggested negative ease.

FINISHED MEASUREMENTS

Bust Circumference: 32 (34.75, 37.25, 41.25, 44, 46.75, 50.75, 53.25)" / 81.5 (88.5, 94.5, 105, 112, 118.5, 129, 135.5) cm.
Length: 24.25 (24.25, 24.75, 25.25, 25.5, 26.5, 26.5, 27.25)"/ 61.5 (61.5, 63, 64, 65, 67.5, 67.5, 69) cm to longest point at back, not including collar.
Size 34.75" / 88.5cm modeled with no ease.

MATERIALS

YARN

Blue Sky Alpacas 'Brushed Suri' (67% Baby Suri, 22% Merino, 11% Bamboo, 130 m / 142 yds per 50g); color: Whipped Cream (900): 5 (6, 6, 6, 7, 7, 8, 8) skeins.

NEEDLES & NOTIONS

US size 10.75 / 7mm circular needle, 16" / 40 cm long for collar
US size 10.75 / 7mm circular needle, 32" / 80 cm long (or longer for bigger sizes)
Set US size 10.75 / 7mm double-point needles (if magic loop is not used for sleeves)
Always use a needle size that gives you the gauge listed, as every knitter's gauge is unique.

Stitch markers, waste yarn, tapestry needle, stitch holder, crochet hook for provisional cast on.

GAUGE

12 sts / 18 rows = 4" / 10 cm in st st

PATTERN NOTES

See techniques section on page 48: Backwards Loop Cast On, Cable Cast On & Provisional Cast On.

PATTERN

I-CORD

CO 3 sts. *K3, sl 3 sts just worked from right to left needle and tug yarn snugly; rep from * until I-cord meas 32 (34, 34, 34, 34, 38, 38, 38)"/ 81.5 (86.5, 86.5, 86.5, 86.5, 86.5, 96.5, 96.5) cm.
K3tog, break yarn, draw yarn tail through final sts.
Tie knot at each end of I-cord.

COLLAR

With shorter circ needles, using Provisional Cast On & waste yarn, CO 60 (64, 64, 68, 68, 76, 76, 76) sts.
With working yarn (leaving 8" / 20.5cm tail) knit 1 row, pm for start of rnd, and join to work in rnd.
Knit 4 rnds.
Turning Rnd: Purl.
Knit 5 rnds.

Joining Rnd: Undo Provisional Cast On, placing resulting sts on longer circ needle. Place first and last 2 sts from cast on onto holder (4 sts total). Fold to form hem at Turning Rnd and hold needle with Provisional Cast On sts at back of work, parallel to working needle. Place I-cord string in pocket with ends hanging out at front. K2 from front needle, *using 1 st from front needle and 1 st from back needle, k2tog; rep from * to last 2 sts, knit 2 sts from front needle.
With tail of yarn BO 4 held cast on sts.
Knit every rnd until neck meas approx 8" / 20.5 cm from

turning rnd.
Set–Up Rnd: K11 (12, 12, 13, 13, 14, 14, 14), pm, k8 (8, 8, 8, 8, 10, 10, 10), pm, k22 (24, 24, 26, 26, 28, 28, 28), pm, k8 (8, 8, 8, 8, 10, 10, 10), pm, knit to end of rnd.
Raglan Inc Rnd: *Knit to m, kfb, sl m, kfb; rep from * 3 more times, knit to end of rnd. 68 (72, 72, 76, 76, 84, 84, 84) sts – *8 sts inc'd.*
Next Rnd: Knit.
Rep these two rnds 11 (11, 11, 11, 11, 12, 12, 13) more times. 156 (160, 160, 164, 164, 180, 180, 188) sts.
Change to longer circ needle when necessary.

For sizes 32 & 34.75" / 81.5 & 88.5 cm proceed to 'All Sizes' below.

Sizes 37.25, 41.25, 44, 46.75, 50.75 & 53.25" / 94.5, 105, 112, 118.5, 129 & 135.5 cm only
Body Inc Rnd: *Knit to m, kfb, sl m, knit to m, sl m, kfb; rep from * once more, knit to end of rnd.
- (-, 164, 168, 168, 184, 184, 192) sts – *4 sts inc'd.*
Next Rnd: Knit.
Rep these two rnds - (-, 0, 1, 2, 2, 4, 4) more times.
- (-, 164, 172, 176, 192, 200, 208) sts.

All Sizes
Knit 8 (10, 10, 10, 10, 10, 8, 10) rnds even. 156 (160, 164, 172, 176, 192, 200, 208) sts total; 32 (32, 32, 32, 32, 36, 36, 38) sleeve sts, 46 (48, 50, 54, 56, 60, 64, 66) front/back sts.

Sleeve Divide Rnd: *Knit to m, remove m, sl next 32 (32, 32, 32, 32, 36, 36, 38) sleeves sts onto waste yarn, remove 2nd m, CO 1 (2, 3, 4, 5, 5, 6, 7) sts using Backwards Loop method, pm for side seam, CO 1 (2, 3, 4, 5, 5, 6, 7) sts; rep from * once more, knit to end of rnd. 96 (104, 112, 124, 132, 140, 152, 160) sts.

BODY
Note: Start of rnd remains in center of front.
Knit even for approx. 2" / 5 cm.
Place dm (dart marker) 16 (17, 19, 21, 22, 23, 25, 27) sts before and after each side m.
Waist Dec Rnd: *Work to dm, sl m, ssk, work to 2 sts before next dm, k2tog, sl m; rep from * once more, work to end of rnd. 92 (100, 108, 120, 128, 136, 148, 156) sts – *4 sts dec'd.*
Rep Waist Dec Rnd every 14 (13, 12, 12, 12, 12, 11, 10)th rnd twice more.
84 (92, 100, 112, 120, 128, 140, 148) sts.
Work even in st st until work meas approx. 10 (9.5, 9, 9, 9, 9, 8.5, 8.25)" / 25.5 (24, 23, 23, 23, 23, 21.5, 21) cm from underarm.
Work to right side seam, sl back 42 (46, 50, 56, 60, 64, 70, 74) sts onto spare needle to be worked later.

Front
Over rem 42 (46, 50, 56, 60, 64, 70, 74) sts, work 2 rows in st st, removing start of rnd m.
Hip Inc Row (RS): Knit to dm, M1R, sl m, knit to next dm, sl m, M1L, knit to end of row. 44 (48, 52, 58, 62, 66, 72, 76) sts – *2 sts inc'd.*
Rep Hip Inc Row every 10th row 2 more times. 48 (52, 56, 62, 66, 70, 76, 80) sts.
Work 9 (9, 11, 11, 11, 13, 13, 13) more rows even in st st. BO all sts.

Back
With circ needle and starting on left side of front 1" / 2.5 cm from bottom edge, pick up and knit 18 (18, 20, 20, 20, 22, 22, 22) sts to beg of held back sts. Knit across 42 (46, 50, 56, 60, 64, 70, 74) held back sts. Pick up and knit down right side of front 18 (18, 20, 20, 20, 22, 22, 22) sts, stopping 1" / 2.5 cm from bottom edge. 78 (82, 90, 96, 100, 108, 114, 118) sts.
Next Row (WS): Purl.
Hip Inc Row (RS): Knit to dm, M1R, sl m, knit to next dm, sl m, M1L, knit to end of row. 80 (84, 92, 98, 102, 110, 116, 120) sts – *2 sts inc'd.*
Work Hip Inc Row every 10th row 2 more times. 84 (88, 96, 102, 106, 114, 120, 124) sts.
Work 9 (9, 11, 11, 11, 13, 13, 13) more rows even in st st. BO all sts.

SLEEVES
Sleeves will be knit in the round using magic loop or dpns. With circ needle (or dpns), starting at center of

47

20 (21.25, 21.25, 22.75, 22.75, 25.25, 25.25, 25.25)" / 51 (54, 54, 58, 58, 64, 64, 64) cm

11.25 (12, 12.75, 13.25, 14, 15.25, 16, 17.25)" / 28.5 (30.5, 32.5, 33.5, 35.5, 38.5, 40.5, 44) cm

9.25 (9.25, 10, 10, 10.75, 11.25, 11.25, 12)"/ 23.5 (23.5, 25.5, 25.5, 27.5, 28.5, 28.5, 30.5) cm

7.25 (7.75, 8.25, 8.75, 9, 9.5, 10, 11)" / 18.5 (19.5, 21, 22, 23, 24, 25.5, 28) cm

Bust

Waist

18 (18, 18.5, 18.5, 19, 19, 19, 19.5)" / 45.5 (45.5, 47, 47, 48.5, 48.5, 48.5, 49.5) cm

17 (16.5, 16.5, 16.5, 17, 17.5, 16.25)" / 43 (42, 42, 42, 43, 42, 41.5) cm

Bust: 32 (34.75, 37.25, 41.25, 44, 46.75, 50.75, 53.25)"/ 81.5 (88.5, 94.5, 105, 112, 118.5, 129, 135.5) cm
Waist: 28 (30.75, 33.25, 37.25, 40, 42.75, 46.75, 49.25)"/ 71 (78, 84.5, 94.5, 101.5, 108.5, 118.5, 125) cm

underarm cast on sts, pick up and knit 1 (2, 3, 4, 5, 5, 6, 7) sts, k32 (32, 32, 32, 32, 36, 36, 38) held sleeve sts, pick up and knit 1 (2, 3, 4, 5, 5, 6, 7) sts from underarm, pm for start of rnd, join to work in the rnd. 34 (36, 38, 40, 42, 46, 48, 52) sts.
Work in st st for 20 (15, 15, 12, 13, 10, 9, 8) rnds.
Sleeve Dec Rnd: K2tog, knit to last 2 sts, ssk. 32 (34, 36, 38, 40, 44, 46, 50) sts - *2 sts dec'd*.
Work Sleeve Dec Rnd every 20 (15, 16, 13, 13, 11, 10, 9)th rnd 2 (3, 2, 2, 4, 4, 1, 3) more time(s) & then every - (-, 15, 12, -, 10, 9, 8)th rnd - (-, 1, 2, -, 1, 5, 4) time(s). 28 (28, 30, 30, 32, 34, 34, 36) sts.
Work even in st st until sleeve meas approx 18 (18, 18.5, 18.5, 19, 19, 19, 19.5)" / 45.5 (45.5, 47, 47, 48.5, 48.5, 48.5, 49.5) cm or desired length from underarm.
BO all sts in pattern.

Finishing

Weave in all loose ends.
Block garment to dimensions given on schematic.

Techniques

Techniques

Cast On Methods

Backwards Loop Cast On
Begin by placing slip knot on your needle. *With working yarn twist loop backwards in yarn, place loop on needle and pull working yarn to tighten stitch up; repeat from * until desired number of stitches have been cast on.

Beaded Cast On
This cast on uses the Long Tail Method but slips a bead between the stitches.
Begin work with a long tail approx. 3 times width of finished dimension. Beads are held on the tail end of yarn.
Create slip knot and tighten on your needle. Keep working yarn to right and yarn tail to left.
With left hand and yarn tail, bring thumb from behind yarn, scoop it up, slide loop created onto needle. Leave thumb in place.
With right hand and working yarn bring yarn around under needle and wrap it on top.
Keep holding this yarn in place.
With left thumb still in first loop, lift this thumb over the end of the needle, scooping the initial loop created over the second loop made. Tighten the ends of the yarn until tension of stitch is correct.
Slip bead up yarn to sit next to stitch just created.
Create 2 more stitches as shown in steps 2-4 then slip new bead up yarn.
Continue to place bead between every 2 sts worked until you have cast on the desired number of stitches.

See http://www.stolenstitches.com/tutorials/knitting-with-beads/long-tail-cast-on-with-beads/ for more.

Cable Cast On
If starting with no stitches on needle, create slip knot, knit into slip knot, place stitch created from right to left needle. *Knit into the gap between the first two stitches, slip new stitch created from right to left needle; repeat from * until desired number of stitches have been cast on. If you are casting on with stitches already on the needle you can begin at *.

See http://www.stolenstitches.com/tutorials/cast-ons/cable-cast-on/ for more.

Provisional Cast On (Crochet Method)
This cast on method uses waste yarn and a crochet hook to create a crochet chain that wraps a stitch around your knitting needle at the same time. It is not necessary to know how to crochet to use this method.
Make a slip knot with waste yarn and place on crochet hook.
Hold crochet hook above the needle; *wrap yarn around and under the needle and then wrap yarn over crochet hook and pull through the stitch on the hook*. There is one stitch on the needle and one stitch on the hook.
Rep from * to * until you have the appropriate number of stitches on the needle.
When you have cast on the correct number of sts, pull end of the yarn through final st on crochet hook and put a knot at end of yarn to mark the end to begin unraveling the chain.
Switch to the project yarn and begin knitting.
When you need to remove the Provisional Cast On, unravel the crochet chain starting at the knotted end. Carefully place each of the live stitches exposed on a needle and begin working as instructed.

See http://www.stolenstitches.com/tutorials/cast-ons/provisional-cast-on-crochet-method/ for more.

Long Tail Cast On

See http://www.stolenstitches.com/tutorials/cast-ons/long-tail-cast-on/ for more.

Bind Off (Cast Off) Methods

I-cord Bind Off
*K2, sl 1 k-wise, k1 (or if no st on needle, pick up and knit stitch from edge of work), psso, sl all 3 sts back on left needle; rep from * until all sts have been worked. Three I-cord sts remain on needle. K3tog, break yarn and draw yarn through final st.

See http://www.stolenstitches.com/tutorials/i-cords/i-cord-bind-off-applied-i-cord/ for more.

3-Needle Bind Off
With right sides of both pieces together, hold the two needles parallel in the left hand, with the WS facing you.

Step 1: Insert the third needle into the first stitch on the front needle and the first stitch on the back needle. Knit these two stitches together.

Step 2: Repeat step 1, then pass the outer stitch on the RH needle over the stitch just made to bind off. Repeat Step 2 until all stitches have been bound off. Cut yarn and pull the tail through the last stitch to secure.

Elastic Beaded Bind Off
16 Color 1 beads must be pre-strung for this Bind Off for Beaded Scarf.
K1, *k1, sl 2 sts to left needle, k2tog tbl, k1, sl 2 sts to left needle, pull bead up to sit at top of yarn behind right needle, k2tog tbl drawing bead through both sts; repeat from * to last st, k1, sl 2 sts to left needle, k2tog tbl, break yarn, draw tail through final st.
Elastic Bind off
K1, *k1, sl 2 sts to left needle, k2tog tbl; repeat from * to end.
If bind off is worked on a purl row, substitute purl for knit.

Other Techniques

Garter stitch
In rows:
Knit all rows

In rnds:
Rnd 1: Knit
Rnd 2: Purl
Rep Rnds 1-2 for pattern.

Grafting
Place an equal number of stitches on the front and back needles; break yarn leaving a generous tail. Thread a tapestry needle with the yarn.

Step 1:
Pull needle through first front stitch as if to purl.
Step 2:
Pull needle through first back stitch as if to knit.
Step 3:
Pull needle through first front stitch as if to knit and slip stitch off needle.
Pull needle through next front stitch as if to purl but leave stitch on needle.
Step 4:
Pull needle through first back stitch as if to purl and slip stitch off needle.
Pull needle through next back stitch as if to knit but leave stitch on needle.
Repeat steps 3 and 4 until all stitches have been worked. Take care to pull yarn carefully through worked stitches periodically. Make sure you do not work it too tight; it should look like a knitted stitch.

Short Rows – W&T Method
On a knit row:
Work the number of sts indicated in the pattern, sl next st purl-wise to RH needle, pass yarn from back to front, slip st back to LH needle. Turn to work purl row, passing yarn to front of work. When you work the next st, take care to pull yarn snugly so there is no gap. Take care not to pull so tightly that you distort the st.

On purl row:
Work the number of sts indicated in the pattern, sl next st purl-wise to RH needle, pass yarn from front to back, slip st back to LH needle. Turn to work knit row, passing yarn to back of work. When you work the next st, take care to pull yarn snugly so there is no gap. Take care not to pull so tightly that you distort the st.

When you come to a wrapped stitch in subsequent rows:
For knit sts: lift the wrap onto the right needle from the front and work it together with the stitch it wraps.
For purl sts: lift the wrap with right needle from the right side of the work and place on the left needle. Work together with the st that was wrapped.

See http://www.craftsy.com/class/short-rows/96 for more.

Short Rows in Garter (W&T)
Work to last st before wrap, sl next st purl-wise from left needle to right needle, bring yarn from back to front of work, sl st back from right needle to left needle. Turn work, yarn is in correct position at back of work. When you work the next st, take care to pull yarn snugly enough that there is no gap. Take care not to pull so tightly that you distort the st.

See http://www.stolenstitches.com/tutorials/short-rows/garter-stitch-short-rows/ for more.

Single Row Buttonhole
Work to buttonhole position: Slip 1 with yarn in front, *slip 1 with yarn in back, pass 1st stitch slipped stitch over 2nd slipped stitch as to bind-off; repeat from * 3 more times, then move resulting stitch back onto left needle.
Turn work; Cast on 5 sts on to left needle using the cable cast-on method.
Turn work again; slip 1 st from left to right needle and pass the last cast-on stitch over it.

I-Cord
*Knit 3 sts, slip 3 sts just worked from right to left needle and tug yarn snugly; repeat from * until I-cord is desired length. To finish, knit three stitches together, break yarn, drawn yarn tail through final stitch.

See http://www.stolenstitches.com/tutorials/i-cords/i-cord/ for more.

Threading Beads onto yarn
Thread sewing needle and create a small knot so that you have a big loop in the thread. Bring tail of your working yarn through this loop so that beads can be threaded directly onto working yarn.
Slip bead onto yarn using sewing needle and all the way down to the working yarn.
If you wish, all beads can be pre-strung before you work or alternatively you can break the yarn before you begin each beaded section to string the beads then.

See http://www.stolenstitches.com/tutorials/knitting-with-beads/pre-stringing-beads/ for more.

ABBREVIATIONS

* *, ()	Repeat instructions between
"	inches
approx	approximately
BO	bind off (cast off)
Cn	cable needle
CO	cast on
cm	centimeter(s)
circ	circular needle
Cont	continue
CC	contrasting color
Dm	dart marker
dec	decrease(ing)
dpn(s)	double pointed needle(s)
est'd	established
g	grams
inc	increase(ing)
k	knit
kfb	knit into front and back of stitch
k3tog	knit 3 stitches together
k2tog	knit 2 together (right-slanting decrease)
k-wise	knit wise
LH	left hand
MC	main color
M1	Make 1: use either M1L, M1R or M1P as needed
M1L	Make 1 Left: Insert LH needle, from front to back, under strand of yarn which runs between next stitch on LH needle and last stitch on RH needle; knit this stitch through back loop.

M1P	Make 1 Purl: Insert LH needle, from back to front, under strand of yarn which runs between next stitch on LH needle and last stitch on RH needle; purl this stitch through front loop.
M1R	Make 1 Right: Insert LH needle, from back to front, under strand of yarn which runs between next stitch on LH needle and last stitch on RH needle; knit this stitch through front loop.
m	marker
m	meter(s) – only used in yarn quantity
meas	measures
mm	millimeters
psso	pass slipped stitch over
patt(s)	pattern(s)
p1b	place 1 bead
p2b	place 2 beads
pm	place marker
prev	previous
p	purl
pfb	purl into the front and back of 1 stitch
p3tog	purl 3 sts together
p2tog	purl two together
p-wise	purl wise
rep	repeat
RH	right hand
RS	right side(s)
rnd(s)	round(s)
sl m	slip marker
sl	slip
sl 1	slip 1 stitch
ssk	slip 2 stitches individually as if to knit, then knit those 2 stitches together through the back loops (left-slanting decrease)

ssp	slip 2 sts individually as if to knit, then purl these 2 stitches together through the back loops.
st(s)	stitch(es)
st st	stockinette stitch (stocking stitch)
tog	together
wyib	with yarn in back
wyif	with yarn in front
w&t	wrap and turn (short row)
WS	wrong side(s)
yd(s)	yard(s)